First World War
and Army of Occupation
War Diary
France, Belgium and Germany

2 CAVALRY DIVISION
3 Cavalry Brigade
Headquarters
4 August 1914 - 30 September 1914

WO95/1130

The Naval & Military Press Ltd
www.nmarchive.com
Published in association with The National Archives

Published by

The Naval & Military Press Ltd

Unit 10 Ridgewood Industrial Park,

Uckfield, East Sussex,

TN22 5QE England

Tel: +44 (0) 1825 749494

www.naval-military-press.com

www.nmarchive.com

This diary has been reprinted in facsimile from the original. Any imperfections are inevitably reproduced and the quality may fall short of modern type and cartographic standards.

© **Crown Copyright**
Images reproduced by permission of The National Archives, London, England, 2015.

Contents

Document type	Place/Title	Date From	Date To
Heading	B.E.F. France & Flanders. Second Cavalry Division 3 Cavalry Brigade. H.Q. 1914 Aug To 1914 Sept.		
Heading	1st Cavalry Division.B.H.Q. 3rd Cavalry Brigade. August 1914		
Heading	War Diary of 3rd Cavalry Brigade From August 4th-August 31st 1914		
War Diary	Curragh	04/08/1914	15/08/1914
War Diary	Dublin	15/08/1914	15/08/1914
War Diary	At Sea	16/08/1914	18/08/1914
War Diary	Havre	18/08/1914	19/08/1914
War Diary	Rouen	19/08/1914	19/08/1914
War Diary	Amiens	19/08/1914	19/08/1914
War Diary	Bussigny	19/08/1914	19/08/1914
War Diary	Maubeuge	19/08/1914	20/08/1914
War Diary	Cousolre	20/08/1914	21/08/1914
War Diary	Solre Sur Sambre	21/08/1914	21/08/1914
War Diary	Merbesle Chateau	21/08/1914	21/08/1914
War Diary	Peissant	21/08/1914	21/08/1914
War Diary	Bray	21/08/1914	22/08/1914
War Diary	9th Kilo Stone W of Bray	22/08/1914	22/08/1914
War Diary	Elouges	23/08/1914	24/08/1914
War Diary	Wargnies	24/08/1914	25/08/1914
War Diary	Le Cateau Catillon	25/08/1914	26/08/1914
War Diary	Homblieres	27/08/1914	27/08/1914
War Diary	Itancourt	27/08/1914	28/08/1914
War Diary	Jussy	29/08/1914	29/08/1914
War Diary	Pierre Mande	30/08/1914	30/08/1914
War Diary	Fontenoy	31/08/1914	31/08/1914
Miscellaneous	Mobilization Orders by Brigadier General H. De la P. Gough, C. B. Commanding 3rd Cavalry Brigade.		
Miscellaneous	Statement showing accommodation Etc., of Personnel & Horses 3rd Cavalry Brigade.		
Miscellaneous	Post Office Telegraphs.		
Miscellaneous	Commanding, 3rd, Cavalry Brigade		
Miscellaneous	No 1 Base Standing Orders For Units Passing Through No 1 Base.		
Operation(al) Order(s)	3rd. Brigade Operation Routine Order No. 1	20/08/1914	20/08/1914
Operation(al) Order(s)	Operation Order No. 1 by Major General E. H. H. Allenby, C.B., Commanding Cavalry Division.	20/08/1914	20/08/1914
Miscellaneous	March Table.		
Operation(al) Order(s)	3rd Cavalry Brigade Operation Order No 2.	20/08/1914	20/08/1914
Miscellaneous	Instructions To Capt Nevi For 210814		
Operation(al) Order(s)	3rd Cavalry Brigade Order No. 3	21/08/1914	21/08/1914
Miscellaneous	Oc 16th Lancers		
Miscellaneous	A Form Messages And Signals		
Operation(al) Order(s)	3rd Cavalry Brigade Order No. 4 Bray	21/08/1914	21/08/1914
Miscellaneous	A Form Messages And Signals.		
Miscellaneous	O.C. Most Western Regiment III Cav. Bde. Bray.		
Miscellaneous	A Form Messages And Signals.		
Miscellaneous	O.C. 5th Lancers Bray		

Miscellaneous	O.C. 5th Lancers	22/08/1914	22/08/1914
Miscellaneous	3rd Cav. Bde.		
Miscellaneous	O C H Squadron	22/08/1914	22/08/1914
Miscellaneous	O.C. A Sqn 4th Hussars		
Operation(al) Order(s)	Operation Order No. 2 by Major General E. H. H. Allenby, C.B., Commanding Cavalry Division.	22/08/1914	22/08/1914
Miscellaneous	A Form Messages And Signals		
Operation(al) Order(s)	Operation Order No. 3		
Miscellaneous	A Form Messages And Signals.		
Miscellaneous	Messages And Signals.		
Miscellaneous	A Form Messages And Signals.		
Miscellaneous	C Form (Original) Messages And Signals.		
Diagram etc	1st Corp HQ. 1 Div HQ		
Miscellaneous	A Form Messages And Signals.		
Operation(al) Order(s)	Operation Order No. 3 by Major-General E. H. H. Allenby, C.B., Commanding Cavalry Division.	29/08/1914	29/08/1914
Operation(al) Order(s)	Operation Order No. 4 by Major General E. H. H. Allenby C. B., Commanding Cavalry Division.	30/08/1914	30/08/1914
Operation(al) Order(s)	1st Army Corps Operation Order No. 4.	30/08/1914	30/08/1914
Miscellaneous			
Miscellaneous	A Form Messages And Signals.		
Operation(al) Order(s)	1st Army Corps Operation Order No. 5.	31/08/1914	31/08/1914
Heading	1st Cavalry Division Transferred About 15th September 1914 to 2nd Cav Division.B. H.Q. 3rd Cavalry Brigade September 1914		
Heading	War Diary 3rd Cavalry Brigade September 1st-September 30th 1914.		
War Diary	Roy St Nicholas	01/09/1914	01/09/1914
War Diary	Antilly	02/09/1914	02/09/1914
War Diary	Villenoy	03/09/1914	03/09/1914
War Diary	Montebise Chateau	04/09/1914	04/09/1914
War Diary	Le Fayet	04/09/1914	04/09/1914
War Diary	Aulnoy	04/09/1914	04/09/1914
War Diary	Chailly	04/09/1914	05/09/1914
War Diary	St Augustin	05/09/1914	05/09/1914
War Diary	Les Bordes	05/09/1914	05/09/1914
War Diary	Vilbert	06/09/1914	06/09/1914
War Diary	Lumigny	06/09/1914	06/09/1914
War Diary	Pezarches	06/09/1914	07/09/1914
War Diary	Paradis	07/09/1914	07/09/1914
War Diary	Epieds	07/09/1915	07/09/1915
War Diary	Mazagran	08/09/1914	08/09/1914
War Diary	Mouroy	08/09/1914	08/09/1914
War Diary	Le Grand Glairet	08/09/1914	09/09/1914
War Diary	Perreuse Chateau	09/09/1914	09/09/1914
War Diary	Rougeville	09/09/1914	10/09/1914
War Diary	Marizy	11/09/1914	11/09/1914
War Diary	Tigny	12/09/1914	12/09/1914
War Diary	Chassemy	13/09/1914	13/09/1914
War Diary	Chateau Chassemy	14/09/1914	14/09/1914
War Diary	Vailly Bridge	14/09/1914	14/09/1914
War Diary	Vailly	14/09/1914	14/09/1914
War Diary	Lime	15/09/1914	30/09/1914
War Diary	Chacrise	30/09/1914	30/09/1914
Operation(al) Order(s)	1st Army Corps Operation Order No. 6.	01/09/1914	01/09/1914
Miscellaneous	Messages And Signals.		

Miscellaneous	A Form Messages And Signals.		
Operation(al) Order(s)	1st Army Corps Operation Order No. 7.	02/09/1914	02/09/1914
Miscellaneous	5 'A' Echelon Will Accompany Brigades.		
Operation(al) Order(s)	Operation Order No. 17 by Field-Marshal Sir John French, G. C. B., Etc., Commanding British Expeditionary Force.	05/09/1914	05/09/1914
Miscellaneous	Operation Routine Order No. 2	07/09/1914	07/09/1914
Operation(al) Order(s)	Operation Order No. 18 by Field-Marshal Sir John French, G. C. B., Etc., Commanding British Expeditionary Force.	07/09/1914	08/09/1914
Miscellaneous	A Form Messages And Signals.		
Operation(al) Order(s)	Operation Order No. 19 by Field-Marshal Sir John French, G. C. B., Etc., Commanding British Expeditionary Force.	08/09/1914	08/09/1914
Operation(al) Order(s)	Operation Order No. 20 by Field-Marshal Sir John French, G. C. B., Etc., Commanding British Expeditionary Force.	09/09/1914	09/09/1914
Miscellaneous	Operation Routine		
Miscellaneous	A Form Messages And Signals.		
Miscellaneous	Messages And Signals.		
Operation(al) Order(s)	Operation Order No. 21 by Field-Marshal Sir John French, G. C. B., Etc.,	10/09/1914	10/09/1914
Operation(al) Order(s)	Operation Order No. 7	13/09/1914	13/09/1914
Operation(al) Order(s)	2nd Army Corps Operation Order No. 23.	13/09/1914	13/09/1914
Operation(al) Order(s)	Operation Order No. 23 by Field-Marshal Sir John French, G. C. B., Etc., Commanding British Expeditionary Force.	12/09/1914	12/09/1914
Miscellaneous	E H Q	13/09/1914	13/09/1914
Miscellaneous	A Form Messages And Signals.		
Operation(al) Order(s)	Operation Order No. 24 by Field-Marshal Sir John French, G. C. B., Etc., Commanding British Expeditionary Force.	13/09/1914	13/09/1914
Miscellaneous	Operation Routine Order No.	14/09/1914	14/09/1914
Miscellaneous	Operation Routine Order No. 8	14/09/1914	14/09/1914
Operation(al) Order(s)	Operation Order No. 24. 2nd Army Corps Headquarters,	13/09/1914	13/09/1914
Miscellaneous	A Form Messages And Signals		
Operation(al) Order(s)	Operation Order No. 25 Field-Marshal Sir John French, G. C. B., Etc., Commander-in-chief, British Forces In The Field.	14/09/1914	14/09/1914
Miscellaneous	A Form Messages And Signals.		
Operation(al) Order(s)	Operation Order No 9		
Miscellaneous	A Form Messages And Signals.		
Operation(al) Order(s)	Operation Order No. 26 by Field-Marshal Sir John French, G C. B., etc., Commander-in-chief, British Forces In The Field.	15/09/1914	15/09/1914
Miscellaneous	3rd Cav. Bde.	19/09/1914	19/09/1914
Operation(al) Order(s)	Operation Orders No.12	17/09/1914	17/09/1914
Operation(al) Order(s)	Operation Orders No. 2 By Brigadier General N. Cough. C.B. Commanding 2nd Cavalry Division,	17/09/1914	17/09/1914
Miscellaneous	O.C. Hussars. 5th Lancers		
Miscellaneous			
Miscellaneous	3rd Brig 5 Brig O.C. R.H.A. OC 4th fd Troop		
Miscellaneous	3rd Cavalry Brigade		
Miscellaneous	Letter Found On German Officer Of VII. Reserve Corps.		

Miscellaneous	3rd Cavalry Brigade
Miscellaneous	A Form Messages And Signals.
Miscellaneous	3rd Cavalry Brigade
Miscellaneous	W.G. 48 Sept. 29
Miscellaneous	
Miscellaneous	A Form Messages And Signals.
Miscellaneous	3rd Bde

B.E.F. FRANCE & FLANDERS.

SECOND CAVALRY DIVISION

3 CAVALRY BRIGADE. H.Q.

1914 AUG TO 1914 SEPT.

1130

B.E.F. FRANCE & FLANDERS.

SECOND CAVALRY DIVISION

3 CAVALRY BRIGADE. H.Q.

1914 AUG TO 1914 SEPT.

1130

1st Cavalry Division

B. H. Q.

3rd CAVALRY BRIGADE.

AUGUST 1914

Army Form C. 2118.

WAR DIARY
or
INTELLIGENCE SUMMARY.

(Erase heading not required.)

Instructions regarding War Diaries and Intelligence Summaries are contained in F. S. Regs., Part II. and the Staff Manual respectively. Title pages will be prepared in manuscript.

Hour, Date, Place	Summary of Events and Information	Remarks and references to Appendices
	CONFIDENTIAL WAR DIARY. of 3rd Cavalry Brigade. From August 4th — August 31st 1914.	

H.Q. 3rd Cav. Brigade.   Army Form C. 2118.

WAR DIARY
or
INTELLIGENCE SUMMARY.

(Erase heading not required.)

Instructions regarding War diaries and Intelligence Summaries are contained in F. S. Regs., Part II. and the Staff Manual respectively. Title pages will be prepared in manuscript.

Hour, Date, Place	Summary of Events and Information	Remarks and references to Appendices
5.20 pm. 4/8/14. CURRAGH.	Received telegram from 'Commander' – MOBILISE.	Informed all Units.
6.0 pm "	Issued 3rd Cav. Bde Mobilisation order.	No 1. Appendix
6.0 pm "	Handed Instructions for Entrainment, etc to Capt Cotgrave - Supply Officer.	RhC
6.40 pm. 5/8/14.	Wired H.Q. "Mobilisation progressing smoothly" 1st Day.	RhC
6.30 pm 6/8/14 "	Wired HQ. "Mobilisation progressing smoothly" 2nd Day. Advanced Party – Supply Details left for SOUTHAMPTON.	RhC
7.5 pm "		RhC
2.30 am 7/8/14.	Received Telegram from H.Q. re Embarkation (No 179)	No 2 Appendix
5.30 pm "	Wired HQ. "Mobilisation progressing smoothly" 3rd day	RhC
5.30 pm 8/8/14.	Wired HQ. "Mobilisation progressing. All horses not drawn yet, difficulty in getting suitable draught horses. Bicycle Covers urgently required and seven bicycles. Brigade Headquarters".	RhC

Army Form C. 2118

WAR DIARY
or
INTELLIGENCE SUMMARY.
(Erase heading not required.)

Instructions regarding War Diaries and Intelligence Summaries are contained in F. S. Regs., Part II. and the Staff Manual respectively. Title pages will be prepared in manuscript.

Hour, Date, Place	Summary of Events and Information	Remarks and references to Appendices
CURRAGH. 9.8.14. 12.30 p.m.	Cavalry Division wired authority to take 1 blanket per mounted man under the saddle, no extra transport being allowed.	No 3. Appendices. Decided to take numnah panels.
6.0 p.m.	Numnah panels being dispensed with at discretion of Brigadier. C.D. 16.	
6.0 p.m.	Wired to Practician to verify day of Movement. Wired to Practician Mobilisation practically complete with following Exceptions — A.S.C. drivers and Police not arrived for Headquarters — Signal Troop wants Shoeing Smith and 3 motor cyclists — 4 th Hussars want Charger and Draught Horses — also Covers for bicycles.	No 4.
6.30 p.m.	Received answer from Practician verifying day of Movement No 406.	No 5.
CURRAGH. 10.8.14. 2.15 p.m.	Cavalry Division asks if purchased horses used are Serviceable.	answered yes.
4.1 p.m.	Coo Dublin will not issue Blankets for men — W.O. letter No 79/5561 dated 7th August.	
5.30 p.m.	Wired Practician — Mobilisation Complete with following Exceptions. Servant for Regl Officer and 4 Drivers for H.R. not arrived. 1 W.N.P. from Aldershot lost on way.	Wired Cavalry Division for authority.
5.45 p.m.	War office wires Rule of Road is to the Right. Wired Practician for Part II Instruction for Short Voyage.	

WAR DIARY
INTELLIGENCE SUMMARY.
(Erase heading not required.)

Army Form C. 2118

Instructions regarding War Diaries and Intelligence Summaries are contained in F.S. Regs., Part II. and the Staff Manual respectively. Title pages will be prepared in manuscript.

Hour, Date, Place	Summary of Events and Information	Remarks and references to Appendices
Curragh. 11/8/14. 11.15 am. 5.30 pm.	Wire from W.O. to Revolved R.H.A. Wire from Cavalry Division to take Bed Blankets. Mobilisation Complete - with following exceptions. O.C. Fd Ambulance. 4 ate Swords & Batmen for Reg officers. 3 motor Cyclists for Signal Troop	See 10/8/14 - 4 pm.
Curragh. 12/8/14. 5.30 pm.	Brigade Mob Complete with exception of 3 motor Cyclists	RMC. RMC.
Curragh. 13/8/14. 3.15 am. 2.30 pm 6 pm.	War has broken out with Austria Hungary (9.643) Brigade Paraded in marching order and Rifle 3rd Cavalry Brigade Mob Complete	No 6 Appendices RMC RMC
Curragh 14/8/14	Portions of the Road Parties of Units started for DUBLIN	
CURRAGH 15/8/14. 5 am.	Headquarters of 3rd Cavalry Brigade. Entrained at Curragh Siding Arrived at NORTHWALL at 6.26 am. Throughout the day all the Railway arrangement made by the G.S. & N. Ry were excellent and punctually carried out. The Naval Transports were not ready for us, and as nearly every horse had to be slung the Embarkation took considerably longer than was expected, and the timetable for the Arrival of Units could not be adhered to. It was also impossible to entrain Units by Train loads	The stalls were too narrow for the horses saddled up.

Army Form C. 2118

WAR DIARY
or
INTELLIGENCE SUMMARY.
(Erase heading not required.)

Instructions regarding War Diaries and Intelligence Summaries are contained in F. S. Regs., Part II. and the Staff Manual respectively. Title pages will be prepared in manuscript.

Hour, Date, Place	Summary of Events and Information	Remarks and references to Appendices
DUBLIN. (Cont'd) 15/8/14	The following was the allotment of Units to Transports.	
	H.Q. 3rd Cav. Bde. & Signal Troop } ATLANTIAN	
	4th Hussars }	
	H.Q. 3rd Bde R.H.A. }	
	16th Lancers } INDIAN	
	Mobile Veterinary Hospital }	
	5th Lancers } KINGSTONIAN.	
	'D' & 'E' Batteries PANCRAS	
	Amm. Column ARCAMEDES	
	Note. There should be more Police at the Dock Gates, and the Quays kept clear of all civilians without passes.	
4.30 pm.	The 5th Lancers left the Port.	
5.30 pm.	'D' & 'E' Batteries " " "	
11.30 pm.	All the Units on the ATLANTIAN were Embarked.	
12 (mn)	" " " INDIAN " "	R.M.C
AT SEA. 16/8/14. 3.20 am	The ATLANTIAN left Port.	Fine day and calm. R.M.C
AT SEA 17/8/14.	Fine day and very calm. Saw from French gunboats near the CHANNEL ISLANDS	R.M.C

WAR DIARY
or
INTELLIGENCE SUMMARY.
(Erase heading not required.)

Army Form C. 2118

Hour, Date, Place	Summary of Events and Information	Remarks and references to Appendices
AT SEA 18/8/14 outside HAVRE. 6.30 a.m. HAVRE. 8.15 a.m.	Picked up Pilot outside HAVRE. (S.S. ATLANTIAN). Made fast to Quay and commenced disembarking. Baggage details to form up in - Every man on board first took his accoutrements on shore and then returned for his saddle, placing them in troops. Then the horses were taken out. From the top deck by horse brand fore and aft. Those from the orlop deck being slung by ropes from one hatch where a horse brand was used. There were no horse brands except a very long one, 4 horse being hoisted in flying to get it down to the lower deck. The vehicles had also been put down a hatch from which the Head Crane could not extract them. They had to be hoisted up by using the ships derricks and then the Cranes.	No 7. Copy of orders for Entrainment attached.
11.45 p.m.	The ATLANTIAN was finished disembarkation, although the four 2 Squadrons of the 5th Hussars were able to catch their trains at 9.30 and 10 p.m. The INDIAN with the 16th Lancers came into dock just after the ATLANTIAN and was disembarked in 3 hours, as trains had been made on board during the voyage. The KINGSTONIAN with the 5th Lancers had arrived overnight, and had proceeded to No 1 Rest Camp.	

Army Form C. 2118.

1st [Cavalry?] [Machine Gun?] and
Sigl M/G [?]

WAR DIARY
or
INTELLIGENCE SUMMARY.
(Erase heading not required.)

Instructions regarding War Diaries and Intelligence Summaries are contained in F. S. Regs., Part II. and the Staff Manual respectively. Title pages will be prepared in manuscript.

Hour, Date, Place		Summary of Events and Information	Remarks and references to Appendices
HAVRE 19/8/14.	4 a.m.	The Brigade entrained during the night for the point of Concentration. The Hd Qrs and 3rd Signal Troop detraining by 4 a.m.	
ROUEN.	10.30 a.m.	Horses watered - and Coffee given to the officers and men.	
AMIENS.	5 p.m.	Horses watered.	
BUSIGNY.	6.45 p.m.	Railway Regulating Station. Received orders to go on to MAUBEUGE and then to march to our billets near COUSOLRE.	
MAUBEUGE.	11 p.m.	Arrived MAUBEUGE and detrained. As it was so late the men were billeted in MAUBEUGE, and the horses picketed.	PMK
20/8/14			
MAUBEUGE.	6.30 a.m.	Got reported to the G.S.O.(I) Cav Div. for any instructions	
	7.15 a.m.	Started for COUSOLRE.	
COUSOLRE.	11 a.m.	Arrived COUSOLRE. Found that Billets had been arranged for the Brigade by Lt Col. GIBBS, & that the 4th Hussars and 5th Lancers had arrived, and that the 16th Lancers arrived	
	12 (noon)	as supply Officer. Capt. COTGRAVE	

Army Form C. 2118.

WAR DIARY
or
INTELLIGENCE SUMMARY.
(Erase heading not required.)

Instructions regarding War Diaries and Intelligence Summaries are contained in F.S. Regs., Part II. and the Staff Manual respectively. Title pages will be prepared in manuscript.

Hour, Date, Place	Summary of Events and Information	Remarks and references to Appendices
COUSOLRE. 20/8/14.	Issued operation order No I	Appendix 8
12.40pm.	Received operation order No I from Cavalry S.S.	9
9 pm	Issued operation order No 2	10
10 pm	with special instructions to reconnoitring Squadron	
COUSOLRE 21/8/14 5.30 am	"A" Sqdn 16th Lancers (Capt. Neave) left for BINCHE.	
" 6.0 am	Remainder of Brigade left for SOIRE SUR SAMBRE	
SOIRE SUR SAMBRE 8.0 am	Arrived Pont 122 between SOIRE SUR SAMBRE & MERBES LE CHATEAU's watered. Advanced guard in Mt MERBER LE CHATEAU, with posts in MERBES Sr MARIE - BIENNE LEZ HAPPART. All clear. Reconnaissance towards LOBBES	
8.20 am	and THUIN - LOBBES Clear. - French Infantry on road from STREE to CHARLEROI.	
9.20 am		
MERBES LE CHATEAU 10 am	left for PEISSANT. Issued operation order No 3.	Appendix 11
PEISSANT 11 am	Brigade arrived less 16th Lancers	
12. (noon)	Received orders for Brigade to go to BRAY at quickly as possible. Issued orders to 16th Lancers calling them in to BRAY.	
1.25 pm	"B" Sqdn from CROIX LES ROUVEROY to ETINNE AU MONT.	
	arrived BRAY. Sent out reconnaissances, and returned	11a
2.30 pm	with 1st Cav.Bde.to left and 5th Cav.Bde.to right at BINCHE	

Army Form C. 2118.

WAR DIARY
or
INTELLIGENCE SUMMARY.
(Erase heading not required.)

Instructions regarding War Diaries and Intelligence Summaries are contained in F. S. Regs., Part II. and the Staff Manual respectively. Title pages will be prepared in manuscript.

Hour, Date, Place	Summary of Events and Information	Remarks and references to Appendices
BRAY — 21/8/14 5/am.	Issued preliminary orders	(12)
7.25 pm.	Issued operation order No 4.	(13)
		BRAY
BRAY 22/8/14 4.30 am	Received order to	(13a)
4.55 am.	Ordered 9th & 5th to stand to in their billets.	(14)
5.45 am.	Informed right flank of 1st Cav Bde of our position — Moved the Brigade out of BRAY to a position of readiness 1½ miles north of BRAY. Towards MAURAGE.	
7.50 am.	Reported position of Brigade to 5th Bde on Right — 1st Bde on Left and to Cav. Div?	(15)
10.30 am.	Reports from patrols up to 10.30 am show that the country up to GOTTIGNIES - ROEULT - HOUDENG AIMERIES was clear of the enemy, but inhabitants all report presence of large forces of the enemy about SOIGNIES and north of LA LOUVIERE — 3rd & 5th Bde RHA arrived.	
10.35 am.	Mayor of BINCHE reported by telephone German force fall around advancing from LA LOUVIERE on TRIVIERES and HAINE ST PAUL and that their Cavalry was already at ST VAST. German guns were seen in action about ST TRIVIERES firing on PERONNES. Sent a squadron 18th Lancers to high ground N-E of BRAY to support the Grays in PERONNES, and brought our artillery up to a position N of TRIVIERES.	
11 am.	'E' Battery came into action against a German battery about TRIVIERES, but could not reach it.	

WAR DIARY
or
INTELLIGENCE SUMMARY.

(Erase heading not required.)

Army Form C. 2118.

Hour, Date, Place	Summary of Events and Information	Remarks and references to Appendices
BRAY. 22/8/14 (cont'd) 11.a.m	Received Cav. Div'l Operation Order No 2 - but no special instructions (mentioned in the order).	
about 12 (noon)	Ordered "A" Echelon back to 9.5 Kilo stone West of BRAY. One or two Squadrons (Scots Greys) came up to "C" Sqdn to support that Squadron which had been driven out of PERONNES. PERONNES village in flames. A section of hostile artillery which had got nearer town unseen, opened on us and put about 20 shells close to the Brigade. There were but and there were no casualties - although the shooting was good. General Allenby arrived, and a little later ordered us to retire. 4th Hussars sent back to behind some factory buildings. 16th Lancers to a lattice just west of BRAY village. "A" Echelon to HARMIGNIES. Later the 5th Lancers Regt 1 Squadron sent back to 9.5 Kilo Stone. 1 Sqdn 4th Hussars left at factory unloading MAURAGE.	
1.15 p.m.	Told 5th Cav Bde we were retiring and that General Allenby wished them to fall back through ESTINNE AUVAL on to the left of the 2nd Cav Bde. Ordered "A" Echelon and Brl Billeting parties back to ÉLOUGES	⑯

[N: R. of Aff 16. C7A]

Army Form C. 2118.

WAR DIARY
or
INTELLIGENCE SUMMARY.
(Erase heading not required.)

Hour, Date, Place	Summary of Events and Information	Remarks and references to Appendices
9.E. Kilo Stone W. of BRAY	22/8/14 1.50pm. The position of the Brigade was as follows:— HQ. 9.E. Kilo Stone. 1 Sqdn 5th Lancers ½ mile N of BRAY intercepts facing E 1 Sqdn 16th Lancers at South of BRAY village. 1 Sqdn 4.th Hussars 1 mile N of 15 Roan facing MAURAGE. Remainder 9.th Hussars and D Battery near factory building. " 5th Lancers ¼ W of 9.E. Kilo Stone " 16.th Lancers just South of 9.E. Kilo Stone. 2pm. Gayl reported they were stirring g of GIVRY 3.30pm. Lt. Tempest-HICKS 16th Lancers was sent out on patrol to clear up the situation on the hill between BRAY and PERONNES and to reconnoitre the latter village. Direction of his patrol is shown on the sketch ——> He found the top of the hill strongly held by Infantry which he practically galloped through. It had his Charger shot under him and lost 2 other horses killed — and 1 man wounded. On attempt made to withdraw off by finding 4pm. a Platoon of Infantry down in BRAY was frustrated by some well directed shells from E Battery. Actual communication established with 5th Bde WR at 3.30pm. MAURAGE reported clear at 3.45pm.	(sketch map showing PERONNES, GIVRY, BRAY, MAURAGE with positions of 5L, 16L, 4H, 9H, HQ, 9.E. Kilo Stone, and I.C.B., with North arrow)

WAR DIARY
or
INTELLIGENCE SUMMARY.
(Erase heading not required.)

Army Form C. 2118.

Hour, Date, Place	Summary of Events and Information	Remarks and references to Appendices
9½ Kilo Stone W. of BRAY 22/8/14 (Contd)	Received Cavalry Div. orders re statement G(a)19.	⑰
4.45 pm	Ordered 4th Hussars to take in their posts.	
4.50 pm	25 German Cavalry holding MAURAGE.	
5.10 pm	Issued orders for the retirement of the Brigade.	
5.30 pm	Sent in to HQ the report of Lieut Hicks reconnaissance.	
6.30 pm	The Brigade retired on to the 4th Cav Bde at NIXERS STEHIAIN. Waited here and at HARMIGNIES. Marched back to ELOUGES via HARVENG — PATURAGES — DOUR. 20 miles along a paved road. A German Airship followed us most of the way.	RNC
23/8/14. ELOUGES 1.40 am	Arrived at ELOUGES (Caus 4 & Hussars) who arrived 2 hours later and went into billets.	
10.30 am	Message from Cav Div. Headquarters that we should probably not leave our Billets today	
	Received orders from Cav Div. to be prepared to move at a moment's notice — on pointing out that the horses would suffer greatly if we were moved today, we received a reply stating that the order was to stand.	
12.20 pm	The men getting tea.	

Army Form C. 2118.

WAR DIARY
or
INTELLIGENCE SUMMARY.
(Erase heading not required.)

Instructions regarding War Diaries and Intelligence Summaries are contained in F.S. Regs., Part II. and the Staff Manual respectively. Title pages will be prepared in manuscript.

Hour, Date, Place	Summary of Events and Information	Remarks and references to Appendices
ELOUGES (Contg) 23/8/14.	The Brigade remained in billets during the rest of the day.	RAC.
ELOUGES. 24/8/14. 4.0 am (very scanty - message lost)	The 3rd Brigade moved our S.W. towards AUDREGNIES, and took up a position of readiness near the Sugar Factory with 1st Cavalry Brigade to our left front near BAISIEUX, and the 4th Cav Bde to our Left Rear. Later on we were all ordered to retire. The 3rd Cav Bde following the 2nd Cav Bde through AUDREGNIES, and halted a mile South on the high ground. A further retirement of the Cavalry Division was ordered, the 3rd Cav Bde remaining as Rear Guard. An officers patrol was sent out to get in touch with the 5th Division near ELOUGES. It was found that they were hard pressed, with a large gap between us. This was reported to the Cav Div. and we started to move nearer. The remainder of the Cav Divs. also came back, the 2nd Cav Bde coming up on our left. All of a sudden they were fired into on their left flank and the battle began. We turned about, all except the 16th Lancers who had gone in in front. We went down towards BAISIEUX, from which place the German Infantry were advancing.	

WAR DIARY
or
INTELLIGENCE SUMMARY.
(Erase heading not required.)

Army Form C. 2118.

Hour, Date, Place	Summary of Events and Information	Remarks and references to Appendices
WARGNIES	The 9th Hussars were ordered to hunt the Infantry, while the 5th Lancers crossed the stream and got up on the high ground on the left. The machine guns of both regiments firing clear the trailing towards BAUSIEUX. Our guns coming into action on the hill behind. The German advance was checked temporarily, the 1st Cav Brigade coming up on the left of the 5th Lancers. Later the Brigade with the remainder of the Division withdrew on AVESNES Station, where the Brigade was collected. There were several casualties, men and horses. Lieuts Faulkner and Pilley 9th Hussars being wounded. Later the whole Division retired to WARGNIES, where we were ordered to take up the infantry trenches, bivouacking on the hill.	
WARGNIES. 25/8/14.	The 3rd Cav Bde moved out with the Remainder of the Cav Div to the S.W. About midday the 16th Lancers had a Squadron in SAULZOIR, the remainder of the Brigade being behind, with the 4.5 Cav. Bde on our left. These two brigades were doing left flank guard to the English Army, with the 1st & 2nd Cav Bdes doing rear guard. All of a sudden the hostile guns opened on and the Division retired being heavily shelled, without firing a shot to near SOLESMES, where we waited massed together expecting to be opened on at any moment. Then we split up into brigades, and towards evening the Brigade retired to WARGNIES.	

WAR DIARY
INTELLIGENCE SUMMARY.
(Erase heading not required.)

Army Form C. 2118.

Hour, Date, Place	Summary of Events and Information	Remarks and references to Appendices
LE CATEAU. CATILLON.	The 3rd Cav Bde first retiring N.E, then E. On our way we were badly shelled by a hostile battery. Major HOCKETT 4th Hussars being wounded. Later we found our way to LE CATEAU, through the 18th Bde. Not knowing what to do we went through LE CATEAU and on to CATILLON, where we billeted for the night. Capt. Bellville 16th Lancers wounded and Lyt. TAULZONR.	RWC
CATILLON. 26/8/14. (map & message cont)	At 9 am we moved out towards LE CATEAU, when we heard, at BAZIEU that the Germans had taken it — we moved up the hill to the left, when we came into action against the German Infantry to cover the retirement of the 5th Division. (Lt. Col. MacLiven 16th Lancers slightly wounded). The Brigade gradually retired on BUSIGNY, where we again tried to cover the retirement of the Infantry. Later we were told to retire on BEAUREVOIR, but finding the roads blocked we retired through the night to HOMBIÈRES, having a 4 hours halt on the way.	

Army Form C. 2118.

WAR DIARY
or
INTELLIGENCE SUMMARY.
(Erase heading not required.)

Hour, Date, Place		Summary of Events and Information	Remarks and references to Appendices
HOMBLIERES	Aug 27th at 9am	3rd Cav Bde order No 5 - (attached). The Brigade moved to HARLY. The Infantry were then retiring through ST QUENTIN. Later hearing that they had all passed through and also the Cavalry, the Brigade retired to Ullers arr d in 3rd Cav Bde order No 6. During the afternoon Lieut J. NOEL. E.YORKS Regt. Came in having escaped from the Germans.	
ITANCOURT	Aug 28th	During the day the Brigade acted as Rearguard, filling the gap between the 1st and 2nd Armies. During the retirement Captain Gatacre (attached to the 4th Hussars) Charged a troop, with a patrol and killed 8 Uhlans. At 11.30 am the G.O.C. sent to Army Headquarters for orders - Cav Bde order No 9. The Brigade billeted about JUSSY.	Copy attached.
JUSSY	Aug 29th	The Brigade retired on CITROUX acting as Rear-guard to the 1st Corps. Early in the morning received G.188 from 1st Corps. At 3.30 pm we received OA 360 from G.H.Q. At this intermittary 12 miles across a country occupied by the Enemy and was 3 hrs not late, the G.O.C would not comply with it.	attached

Army Form C. 2118.

WAR DIARY
or
INTELLIGENCE SUMMARY.
(Erase heading not required.)

Instructions regarding War Diaries and Intelligence Summaries are contained in F.S. Regs., Part II. and the Staff Manual respectively. Title pages will be prepared in manuscript.

Hour, Date, Place	Summary of Events and Information	Remarks and references to Appendices
Aug. 29th (contd).	Received G.C. 29 from 1st Corps. (attached) The Brigade went into Billets just S. of CHAUNY.	
PIERRE MANDÉ. Aug. 30th 2 am. 3.30 am.	Issued 3rd Cav Bde order No 8. (attached) The Brigade marched to protect the left flank of the 1st Corps. During the morning received G.C. 33 from 1st Corps (attached) During the day received G. 105 from Cav Div.n ordering the Brigade to RETHONDES (on the other flank of the Army Corps) also G. 215 from 1st Corps. The Brigade billetted just north of the River about FONTENOY.	attached
FONTENOY. Aug. 31st 5.50 pm.	Remained in billets till midday, when the advance of hostile Cavalry was reported. The Brigade crossed the River at FONTENOY, the rear guard being hard pressed. Issued orders for billets - BM 10. 31/8/14 (attached)	

MOBILIZATION ORDERS

BY

BRIGADIER GENERAL H. DE PA P. GOUGH, C.B.

Commanding 3rd Cavalry Brigade.

∗∗∗

Curragh, 4th August, 1914.

1. The order to mobilize has been received. Tomorrow the 5th day of August, 1914, will be the first day of mobilization.

2. Lieut. G.F.H.Brooke, 16th Lancers, is appointed Staff Captain and will join for duty before noon on the 3rd day.
   Lieut. E.Ramsden, 5th Lancers is appointed A.D.C. and Camp Commandant, and will join for duty at once.
   Lieut. B.W.Robinson, 5th Lancers is appointed Brigade Machine Gun Officer, and will receive further instructions as to when and where he will join the Brigade Headquarters.

3. The unit at Stewart Barracks will furnish a Horse Conducting Party to draw horses for Brigade Headquarters. Numbers as below:-
   Officers Horses, 9 (G.O.C.5, B.M.2, S.C.1, A.D.C.1.)
   Troop Horses,   7 (M.M.P.),
   Draught Horses, 8.(A.S.C.).

4. The Personnel of Brigade Headquarters will be attached to Units in accordance with the detail shown in Appendix A, until further orders.

5. All men attached to Brigade Headquarters will report themselves to the Camp Commandant at Brigade Office at 6 p.m. tomorrow.

6. Officers of the Headquarters will be medically inspected at 8 a.m. at the Medical Inspection room West Wing, or the Barrack room adjacent, on the 1st day of mobilization. The batmen of the officers of the Headquarters will be medically examined with Squadrons of their own units.

7. Horses on the peace establishment of Brigade Headquarters will be sent for inspection to the Riding School, Stewart Barracks at 12 noon, on the 1st day of mobilization.
   Horses passed fit will be shod at 3 p.m. on that day at Stewart Barracks.

8. All passes are withdrawn from this date.

9. All documents of the personnel detailed to join Headquarters will be forwarded to the Brigade Office not later than 12 noon on the 3rd day of mobilization.

10. All N.C.O's and men (including Officers' chargers and all other horses) of the 3rd Cavalry Brigade Headquarters will parade in service dress marching order at 3 p.m. on the 5th day of mobilization in front of the Brigade Office.

11. The Unit at Stewart Barracks will be responsible for alloting a room in its barracks as a store room for Headquarters.

12. The 3rd Signal Troop R.E. will be responsible for:-
   (i) Drawing (and marking) of War Equipment for Brigade Headquarters (Mob.Regns. para:17 b.) at 8 am on the 1st and 2nd days of mobilization from the Ordnance, Curragh.
   (ii) Indenting for and drawing at 9 a.m. on the 2nd day of mobilization the supplies according to the Office Memo:No. 29/268 of the 19/9/11.
   iii. On the 6th day of mobilization, detailing parties to collect, load and entrain Headquarter baggage under instructions which will be issued by the Camp Commandant.
   iv. On the 6th day of mobilization, returning to the Ordnance, Curragh, articles already drawn to supplement barrack equipment.

13. The A.D.C. and Camp Commandant will take over the War Equipment from the 3rd Signal Troop R.E. and hand over to the drivers supplied by the A.S.C. the vehicles, harness, horses, etc, of the train.

14. The 3rd Signal Troop R.E. will mount a sentry over the Headquarter store room abovementioned on the 1st day of mobilization.

15. Kits to be left at the Base to be handed over to the O.C. Base Details, Stewart Barracks on the 6th day of Mobilization.

16. Units will report progress at 5 p.m. daily. They will also report the moment their mobilization is complete.

17. From today inclusive, Brigade Headquarters will be open day and night. Units will arrange to have a bicycle orderly on duty at this Office both by day and night.

Statement showing accommodation etc., of Personnel & Horses
3rd Cavalry Brigade.

Detail.	Servants	Furnished by unit in	NCOs	Men	Horses	Where accommodated	To whom attached for rations, pay, shoeing, etc.	Day required to join	Day leaving Curragh	Remarks.
G.O.C.	3	1, Marlborough 2, Ponsonby Bks	---	3	5	Brownstown Ho.	Unit, Stewart Bks Unit, Ponsonby "	1st	7th	
Brigade Major.	2	Stewart Bks.	---	2	3	Athgarvan Ldge	Unit, Stewart Bks	1st	7th	
Staff Captain.	2	Ponsonby " Bks.	---	2	3	Ponsonby Bks.	Unit, Ponsonby "	3rd 12 noon.	7th	
A.D.C. (Camp Cmdt.)	2	Marlborough	---	2	3	Stewart Bks.	Unit, Stewart Bks	1st	7th	
Bde. M.G. Officer.	2	Own Unit.	---	2	3	Own Unit.	Own Unit.	1st	7th	
Clerk to Staff.	---	A.S.C.	1	---	---	A.S.C. Bks.	A.S.C.	1st	7th	
Mil. M. Police.	---	3 from Curragh) 7 " Aldershot.)	1	9	10	3 in M.P.Bks. (4 Ponsonby, (3 Stewart Bks	M.M.P.Curragh) A, Ponsonby Bks.) B, Stewart Bks.)	12 noon 5th	7th	
Army Post O.Corps.	---	---	1	2	---	Stewart Bks.	Unit, Stewart Bks	12 noon 6th	7th	
Cook.	---	Stewart Bks.	---	1	---	Stewart Bks.	Unit, Stewart Bks.	1st	7th	

A.

Prefix _____ Code _____

Office of Origin and Service Instructions.

SEE NOTICE AT BACK.

POST OFFICE TELEGRAPHS.
(Inland Telegrams.)

Words. _____ Sent
Charge. _____ At _____ M.
_____ To _____
_____ By _____

No. of Telegram _____

For Postage Stamps.
To be affixed by the Sender.
Any Stamp for which there is not room here should be affixed at the back of this form.

A Receipt for the Charges on this Telegram can be obtained, price one Penny.

When a reply is to be prepaid, write the words "Reply Paid" in the space below. These words are not charged for.

12 words, including the words in the address, 6ᴅ.
Every additional word, ½ᴅ.

TO { Brigadier Cavalry Curragh

179	Aug 6th	Embark	Expeditionary	Force
less	fourth	and	first	divisions
AAA	First	day	movement	in
Expeditionary Force	Railway	Table		
will	be	August	ninth	acknowledge

FROM { Practician — Dublin.

The Name and Address of the Sender, IF NOT TO BE TELEGRAPHED, should be written in the Space provided at the Back of the Form.

(This Paper Manufactured and Printed by McCORQUODALE & CO. Limited.) Wt. 6892/294. 7—8/12. 25,500,000. Sch. 2.

(2)

POST OFFICE TELEGRAPHS

N.B.—This Form must accompany any inquiry respecting this Telegram.

If the Receiver of an Inland Telegram doubts its accuracy, he may have it repeated on payment of half the amount originally paid for its transmission, any fraction of 1d. less than ½d. being reckoned as ½d.; and if it be found that there was any inaccuracy, the amount paid for repetition will be refunded. Special conditions are applicable to the repetition of Foreign Telegrams. Office of Origin and Service Instructions.

Office Stamp: CURRAGH AU 9 14 C.

Charges to pay: s. d.

Handed in at Aldershot 11 —— Received here at 2.30 p.m.

TO { Brigadier Cavalry Aldershot

C 22 D 16 tents on point blanket will be issued to take by mounted men of Cavalry and camel under saddle at the station transport allowed a. a. a.

③

POST OFFICE TELEGRAPHS.

T.B.—This Form must accompany any inquiry respecting this Telegram.

If the Receiver of an Inland Telegram doubts its accuracy, he may have it repeated on payment of half the amount originally paid for its transmission, any fraction of 1d. less than ½d. being reckoned as ½d.; and if it be found that there was any inaccuracy, the amount paid for repetition will be refunded. Special conditions are applicable to the repetition of Foreign Telegrams.

Office of Origin and Service Instructions.

Charges to pay: s.

Handed in at ... .M., Received here at ... .M.

Office Stamp.

TO {

(2) Brigade may be despatched at discretion of Brigadier
Commander Cavalry Division

POST OFFICE TELEGRAPHS.
(Inland Telegrams.)

A.
Prefix ____ Code ____
Office of Origin and Service Instructions.

Words ____ Sent
Charge ____ At ____ M.
To ____
By ____

No. of Telegram ____

For Postage Stamps.
To be affixed by the Sender.

Any Stamp for which there is not room here should be affixed at the back of this form.

A Receipt for the Charges on this Telegram can be obtained, price one Penny.

(4.)

When a reply is to be prepaid, write the words "Reply paid" in the space below. These words are not charged for.

TO { Tactician Dublin

C.1.

Reference	your	179	August 6th
understand	from	fifth	division that
day	of	movement	Cavalry
Brigade	will	for	Fourteenth
is	this	August	Present
	correct		

one seven nine   sixth

FROM { Brigadier Cavalry.

The Name and Address of the Sender, IF NOT TO BE TELEGRAPHED, should be written in the Space provided at the Back of the Form.

(This Paper Manufactured and Printed by McCORQUODALE & CO. Limited.)   Wt. 6322/584. 7—3/12. 24,500,000. Sch. 2.

A.
Prefix _____ Code _____
Office of Origin and Service Instructions.

Meerut 10/30 hr 9/8/14

SEE NOTICE AT BACK
POST OFFICE TELEGRAPHS.
(Inland Telegrams.)

Words. _____ Sent

Charge. | At _____ M.
| To _____
| By _____

No. of Telegram _____
For Postage Stamps.
To be affixed by the Sender.
Any Stamp for which there is not room here should be affixed at the back of this form.
A Receipt for the Charges on this Telegram can be obtained, price one Penny.

(5)

When a reply is to be prepaid, write the words "Reply paid" in the space below. These words are not charged for.

TO { 3rd Cavalry Brigade
      Amagh

No. A66	you	Col	9/8/19
yes	day	of	movement for
Cavalry	Bde	is	Istant

12 words, including the words in the address,
6D.
Every additional word,
½D.

FROM { Practical

The Name and Address of the Sender, IF NOT TO BE TELEGRAPHED, should be written in the Space provided at the Back of the Form.

(This Paper Manufactured and Printed by McCORQUODALE & CO. Limited.) Wt. 5932/394. 7—9/12. 25,500,000. Sch. 2

POST OFFICE TELEGRAPHS.

Handed in at 9.30 a.m. Received here at 3.6 p.m.

From Dublin

TO G.O.C. 3rd Cavalry Bde Curragh

9.643 August 13th war has broken out with Austria Hungary all stations in Ireland informed acknowledge

Commander-in-Chief

(6)

G. Commanding, 3rd Cavalry Brigade

Please note that the Brigade under your command will entrain as detailed below :—

The time given is the hour at which units are to be at "point" specified.

An officer from each unit Should reconnoitre the road to the place of entrainment and report at the Headquarter Office No. 1 Base, QUAI DES TRANSATLANTIQUES (Telephone No. 23), where " points " referred to below will be shewn them from the map.

(1) 3rd Cavalry Brigade

A Cavalry Regt. H.Q. (less interpreters horse). also 1 squadron at 9.30 p.m. at point No. 6, south of the HANGAR AUX COTONS
(2) Machine Gun Section (plus interpreters horse) also 1 squadron at 10 p.m. 18th August at point No. 7 South of the QUAI DE SAIGON
1 Squadron at 2 a.m. 19th August at point No. 4 GARE DES MARCHANDISE

B Cavalry Regiment. H.Q. (less interpreters horse) also 1 squadron at
(3) 10 p.m. 18th August at point No. 8 South of the QUAI DE LA PLATA
Machine Gun Section (plus interpreters horse) also 1 squadron at 11.30 p.m. 18th August at point No. 2 GARE DES MARCHANDISE
(4) 1 Squadron at 3 a.m. 19th August at point No. 9. GARE DE TRIAGE.

C. Cavalry Regiment. H.Q. (less interpreters horse) also 1 squadron at 6.45 a.m. 19th August at point No. 2 HANGAR AUX COTONS
Machine Gun Section (plus interpreters horse) also 1 squadron at 9 a.m. 19th August at point No. 1 GARE DES MARCHANDISE
1 Squadron at 12.15 p.m. 19th August, at point No. 5, on the south side of the HANGAR AUX COTONS.

3rd Cav. Bde Headquarters and 3rd Signal Troop at 2 a.m. 19th August at point No. 4 GARE DES MERCHANDISE.

As "C" Regt are in No 1 Camp separate orders will be sent them.

Havre
18/8/14

E Montagu

The entrance to points Nos. 1, 2, and 4 is at No. 70 Cour de la Republique.

Units will draw supplies from the main Supply Depot 6 hours before time of entrainment. Transport will be supplied at the main Supply Depot for the conveyance of these supplies to the point of entrainment. [HANGAR AUX COTONS] This transport must not be kept at the point of entrainment by units longer than it is absolutely necessary as it is required by other units also entraining.

All units must send a representative to the HANGAR AUX COTONS, who is capable of directing the transport to the point of entrainment.

No 1 Base.

Standing Orders for Units passing through No 1 Base.

1. The Base Commandant is the sole channel of communication between the British and French Authorities. All British demands on the French Authorities for extra transport, labour, billets, buildings, requisitions, &c must be made through him.

2. Officers must impress on their men the necessity of showing the utmost courtesy to the inhabitants whether officials or civilians. Rank and file will salute all French Naval and Military Officers.

3. <u>Entrainment</u>. Units will be informed by the Base Commandant of the date, hour and place of entrainment. It is absolutely essential that strict punctuality is observed in all entraining arrangements, and O.C. Units are responsible that the route to the place of entrainment is reconnoitred by an Officer during the day in Camp. Units proceeding to Rest Camps will invariably give way to those proceeding to place of entrainment.

4. <u>Discipline - Passes</u>. No soldier below the rank of SERJEANT will be allowed into HAVRE except on duty. Serjeants and N.C.O's above that rank must be in possession of a pass signed by their Commanding Officer.

5. <u>Disembarkation States</u>. All Units or detachments disembarking will render to the MILITARY LANDING OFFICER returns and nominal roll of officers.

6. <u>Camp Accommodation - Scale of</u>.- Tents are calculated for at the following rates:—
   General or Field Officers — — — — 1
   3 Other Officers — — — — — — 1
   12 Other Ranks — — — — — — 1

(4)

7. Interpreters. — ~~During their stay in camp units~~ will be joined by their Interpreters.

8. Guides. Units will be furnished with a Guide by the Military Landing Officer and informed by him of the number of the Camp which they are to occupy.

9. Transport. — Units will arrange to utilize their own transport for any service which may be required by them.

In the case of units not equipped with transport, it will be provided to convey baggage from the Dock to Camp, and from Camp to place of entrainment; also to draw supplies.

All units will be provided with extra transport to assist them to convey rations, required for the Rail journey, to the station.

O.C. units will notify their requirements in transport for this service to the M.L.O. on the landing stage, as early as possible.

10. Supplies. (i) Units will draw ONE day's (complete) supplies and forage in Camp.

(ii) They will also draw any additional supplies which may be required to enable them to entrain with the following —

(a) ONE day's cooked ration in the cookers and on the man for the railway journey.

(b) ONE day's preserved meat and biscuit &c. on the man for the day of or after detrainment.

(c) Usual reserve ration in own transport with un

11. Medical. All Medical Officers i/c units disembark will render a 'state' of sick of their units to the Disembarking Medical Officer immediately on arrival. Only cases requiring to be left at the base will be included on this return.

12. Sanitary. Latrines will be disinfected with Lime each day. The lime will be supplied by the Base Sanitary Authorities.

13. The Headquarters of the Base Commandant is situated at the Dock Offices of the Compagnie Generale Transatlantique, The Quai Transatlantique.

14. Milk - The use of milk by men, unless tinned, is STRICTLY PROHIBITED, owing to the prevalence of enteric fever in the district.

15. Maps - Maps will be issued to O.C. Units by the M.L.O. and they will be taken on to the Concentrative Camp.

16. O.C. Units will send 1 Senior Officer, the Transport Officer and, if possible, the Transport Serjeant also, to report to the O.C.D. Railway Transport at his office on the Main Platform of the Gare des Voyageurs early on the day following disembarkation.

17. The Advance Party, as laid down in para. 13, Instructions for Entrainment and Embarkation of Troops (Short Voyage) Part II, will report to the Railway Transport Office at the entraining point 2 hours before their unit is ordered to be there.

18. Instructions for Entrainment and Embarkation (Short Voyage) Part II must be rigidly adhered to, particularly those portions referring to entrainment of horses.

19. The ropes referred to in para (c) of the above Regulation as required for the entrainment of horses must be improvised by tying 2 picketting ropes together, which must be kept ready for this purpose; 4 such ropes will be required for every 8 horses.

20. All horses will travel unsaddled.

21. All A.S.C. Officers arriving with transport proceeding by road will report, on arrival to D.A.D.T at the offices of the Compagnie Generale Transatlantique, The Quai Transatlantique.

22. Money Changing of - The following rate of exchange has been fixed at HAVRE — £1 = 25 francs, 1 shilling = 1 franc 20 centimes, 1 penny = 10 centimes. Soldiers should be warned not to part with their money at less rates. It is known that they have been parting with sovereigns at a loss of 10 frs to each sovereign.

(sd) E. Montague. Colonel.

Copy No. (8)3

3rd Brigade {Operation / Routine} Order No. 1

COUSOLRE.
20/8/14.

Reference Map 1/100,000

1. The Brigade will billet tonight in and around COUSOLRE.

2. <u>Standing Posts</u>, dismounted with rifles will be placed immediately on all roads leading out of billets.
<u>Mission</u>. Stop <u>all</u> persons, examine them and send all suspicious persons to Bde HdQrs. An interpreter with each post day and night.

  <u>4th Hussars</u>. Roads leading to ~~REUGNIES~~, REUGNIES and MAREIGNY.
  <u>16th Lancers</u>. Roads leading to BERSILLIES-L'ABBAYE and MAUBERGE. (BOUSIGNIES)
  <u>5th Lancers</u>. Roads leading to AIBES, BERELLES - FESTRUD.

3. <u>At night</u> - all roads into billets to be blocked, but passage allowed through, with lights kept on them and sentry in front.
<u>Mission</u> - defend it, if necessary.

4. The following observation posts, with glasses and signallers, will stay out till 8 pm.

Copy No.

Operation } Order No.
Routine }

Reference
          on road
(a) at wood, just N.E of MAREIGNY, looking towards LEUGNIES. (4th Hussars).
(b) about Pt 220 looking towards
   ① BERSAILLES L'ABBAYE.
   ② BEAUMONT.
found by 16th Lancers.

5. The following officers patrols with Interpreters will start at 4 pm - mission to obtain touch with Frontier Guards and report presence of allied troops or news of enemy.
① 16th Lancers. to BERSAILLES L'ABBAYE and BOUSIGNIES.
② 4th Hussars. to CHAUDEVILLE and LEUGNIES.
③ 5th Lancers. to WARENNES and FESTRUD.

Note. The SOLRE - BEAUMONT - CHARLEROI Road is not to be touched by our troops.

6. Squadron officers will reconnoitre perimeter of billets with a view to defence and inform their subordinates of plans.

7. All sentries will have their rifles loaded, but will withhold their fire.

Copy No.

Operation / Routine Order No.

Reference

8. Wine shops and restaurants are not put out of bounds, but they will be watched by the M.M.P and if they are abused they will be immidiately put out of bounds.

9. Men will salute all officers of our allies, and will ~~salute~~ in a friendly and courteous manner their comrades of the French and Belgian armies.

10. No aeroplanes will be shot at, but ZEPPELIN air ships may be shot at.

11. Protection of the Transport on the march. Every man with the transport will carry his rifle slung on his back. All distinguishing flags will have their numerals or letterings removed.

12. All papers not required are to be burnt, and men are to be warned against talking to inhabitants about any moves.

Copy No. **10**

Operation / Routine } Order No.

Reference

13. Reports to the MAIRIE - COUSOLRE.

14. Units will be ready to march at 7 am tomorrow.

            R J Kearsley Major.
                       Bm:
              3rd Cav: Bde

Issued at 12.40 pm.
   Copy No 1 to O.C. 4th Hussars personally
     " " 2 " " 16th Lancers   "
     " " 3 " " 5th   " bicycle orderly
     " " 4 " " 3rd Signal Tp. personally.

Copy No: 3

OPERATION ORDER No.1
by
Major General E.H.H. ALLENBY, C.B., Commanding Cavalry Division.

20th August, 1914.

1. (a). Small parties of the enemy may be expected from the north east.

   (b). The 5th Cavalry Brigade is attached to the Division.

2. The Division will march to-morrow in accordance with the attached March Table.

3. The 3rd Brigade will detail a squadron to march at 5.30 a.m. on BINCHE to reconnoitre that town and report if it is held by the Belgians or not. It will rejoin its Brigade when relieved by 5th Cavalry Brigade.

4. Brigades will be responsible for the outpost sections as follows :-

   3rd Brigade
      MERBES-le-CHATEAU to cross roads at 19th kilo stone south of BINCHE inclusive.
   5th Brigade.
      19th kilo stone exclusive to the cross roads at the 13th kilo stone west of BINCHE exclusive.
   1st Brigade.
      continue the line to MONS Exclusive.

5. Reports to the cross roads one mile north west of JEUMONT until 8 a.m., after that hour to the cross roads one half mile south east of GIVRY.

Issued at 7-30 p.m.

J. VAUGHAN. Colonel, G.S.

MARCH TABLE.

Unit.	Starting Point.	Time.	Route.	Destination.
1st Brigade.	x-roads N.W. of MARPENT.	7 a.m.	GRAND RENG - ROUVEROY - HARMIGNIES.	St.SIMPHORIEN. VILLERS-St-GHISLAIN.
H.A. (less A.C.) Signal Squadron. Field Squadron R.E.	x-roads one mile north of AIBES.	6.15.	JEUMONT, and follow 1st Brigade.	GIVRY.
2nd Brigade.	x-roads half mile N.E. of OBRECHIES.	6.15	QUIEVELON - AIBES. To follow Field Squadron R.E. To follow 2nd Brigade.	HARVENG & HARMIGNIES. ROUVEROY & CROIX-lez-ROUVEROY.
4th Brigade.	x-roads WATTIGNIES.	6.15		HAULCHIN - FAUROEULX.
3rd Brigade.		5.30	MERBES-le-CHATEAU - PEISSANT - CROIX-le-ROUVEROY.	BINCHE.
5th Brigade.	x-roads LES GRAVETTES.	7.15	FERRIERE-la-Gde - CERFONTAINE - COLLERET - JEUMONT - MERBES-le-CHATEAU. 1¾ miles east of COLLERET.	GIVRY.
3rd Field Amb.	Head at x-roads 1¼ miles E. of COLLERET.	7.30	To follow 4th Brigade.	GIVRY.
1st Field Amb.	Head at x-roads in JEUMONT.	8.15	To follow 3rd Field Ambulance.	
			"B" ECHELON. 1st line TRANSPORT.	
1st Brigade.	x-roads north west of MARPENT.	7.30	VILLERS-sire-NICOLE - GIVRY - HARMIGNIES.	VILLERS-St-GHISLAIN and St.SYMPHORIEN.
Headquarters. 3rd Bde.Amm.Col. 7th Bde.Amm.Col. Field Squadron Signal Squadron	T-roads just east of QUIEVELON.	7.30	COLLERET - MARPENT - VILLERS-sire-NICOLE. QUIEVELON; follow Signal Sqdn: "B" echelon.	GIVRY.
2nd Brigade.	x-roads half mile north east of OBRECHIES.	7.30	OBRECHIES; follow 2nd Bde.	HARMIGNIES.
4th Brigade.			Follow 3rd Bde to the INN near the 23rd kilo stone on BEAUMONT - MONS road, via main road to ROUVEROI.	ROUVEROI.
3rd Brigade.	End T in WATTIGNIES	7.30		FAUROEULX & HAULCHIN.

Copy No. 8

3rd Cavalry Brigade
Operation order No 2.

⑩

Ref. NAMUR. sheet 8.
1/100,000

COUSOLRE
20th Aug. 1914.

1/(A). Small parties of the enemy may be expected from the N.E.

(B). Cavalry division marches north tomorrow, through MARPENT — GRAND RENG — ROUVROY to the area ST. SYMPHORIEN — GIVRY.

(C). The 5th Cavalry brigade is attached to the division and marches via JEUMONT — MERBES LE CHATEAU — BINCHE.

2/. The task of the 3rd Cav. brigade is to act as right flank guard to the division

3/. In consequence brigade will

will march via BERSILLIES
L'ABBAYE — SOLRE SUR SAMBRE
on MERBES LE CHATEAU where
a halt will be made.
Starting point. Cross roads where
the road BERSILLIES L'ABBAYE
leaves the COUSOLRE — BEAUMONT
road. at 6:15 a.m.
Order of march.
  Advanced guard. (Col. MACEWEN).
    16th Lancers (less 1 squadron).
  Main Body.
    Head Quarters.
    5th Lancers
    4th Hussars (less ½ squadron).
    Brigade Machine guns (less section
                                           16th Lancers)
  ("A" Echelon 1st Line transport.
          (order of march 16th H.Q. 5th.
   under Capt. W. Gibbs 10th Hussars 4th)

"B" Echelon 1st Line transport.
(16th. H.Q. 5th. 4th.)
under Capt. Bridge I.A.

Rear Guard.
2 troops 4th Hussars.

On arrival at MERBES LE CHATEAU the O.C. Advanced Guard will occupy MERBES STE MARIE with half a squadron which will send a standing patrol into BIENNE LES HAPPART.

4/. O.C. 16th Lancers will detail one squadron to march at 5.30 a.m. under special instructions to be issued to the squadron commander.

5/ "B" Echelon 1st Line transport (less that of 16th Lancers) will on arrival at the INN near 23rd stone BEAUMONT — MONS road turn up up the main road to ROUVEROY and thence to CROIX-LES-ROUVEROY and park off the road awaiting orders.

6/ Reports to head of main body.

7/ In future all chin straps will be worn under the chin;

all men on bicycles will carry their rifles slung on their backs.

Issued at
9.40 pm

R. H. Cauley
Bde. Major.
3rd Cavalry Brigade

Copy No 1 4th Hussars
"   " 2 5th Lancers
"   " 3 16th Lancers
"   " 4 O.C. 1st Line Transport.
"   " 5 Bde. Machine Gun officer
"   " 6 3rd Signal Troop.
"   " 7 Capt Bibbs.
"   " 8 to keep.
"   " 9 Supply officer.

Instructions to Capt Neam. for 24.8.14

1.) Reconnoitre Binche, & hold it till relieved by 5th Brigade, starting at 5.30. a.m.

2.) Push a patrol via Bousignies-Leers et Fosteau - Lobbes - to X roads, 1 mile west of Fontaine l'Eveque -
Negative information required from (a) Fontaine Valmont to Main body at Solre ~~sur~~. Merbes le château
(b) from Lobbes, - to Main body at Merbes Ste Marie -
If all clear at Fontaine d'Eveque, patrol rejoins Squadron at Binche.

3.) French Cav Corps of 3 Divisions was at Gembloux yesterday, but fell back South
2 Divisions German Cav. reported at Braine d'Alleud - at 11. a.m. yesterday (23 miles N.E. of Binche)

4.) Cav Div marches to area St Symphorien - Givry.
3rd Cav Brig acts as Right Flank Guard, has a long halt at Merbes -le- château, & billets about Haulchin - Jauroeulx.
5th Brig moving on Binche through Merbes -le- château, may arrive Binche about 12 noon.

5.) Reconnoitre outside Binche, upto 3 miles N. & N.E, & E. - before arrival of 5th Brigade.

HPG.

Copy No. 11

3rd Cavalry Brigade Order No 3
MERBES LE CHATEAU
21/8/14

Namur Map.

1. At 9.30 am the Brigade (less 16th Lancers) will continue its march via PEISSANT and CROXX-LES-ROUVEROY to its billeting area HAULCHIN and FAUROEULX.
Order of march.
Advanced Guard.   1 Sqdn 5th Lancers.
Main Body   H.Qrs
                   5th Lancers (less 1 Sqdn)
                   Bde Machine Guns (less 16th Lancers)
                   4th Hussars (less 2 Troops)
                   'A' Echelon 1st L.T.
Rear Guard.   2 Troops 4th Hussars

2. The 16th Lancers will be responsible for the outpost section as follows.
MERBES-LE-CHATEAU to Cross roads at 19th Kilo stone South of BINCHE inclusive, linking up with 5th Cav: Bde at latter place.
The H.Q. 16th Lancers and reserve (at least 1 Squadron) will be at PEISSANT.
The O.C. 16th Lancers will make his dispositions as soon as the remainder of the Brigade has passed through MERBES LE CHATEAU.
He will keep two standing patrols
① at LOBBES ② at Cross roads

PLEIN DE CHENES. to remain out till 5 am, unless relieved beforehand.

3. 'A' Echelon 16th Lancers 1st L.T. has been ordered to report to O.C. 16th Lancers at MERBES LE CHATEAU at once, and orders have been sent to 'B' Echelon 16th Lancers to go to MERBES LE CHATEAU.

4. Repats to Head of Main Body.

Issued at 9.20 am.

R M Cearley Major
BM. 3CB.

(11a)

O.C. 16th Lancers.   HERBES STE MARIE
BM4 – 21/8/14.

1. German Cavalry marching from direction NIVELLES on MONS and may be expected on the line of the CANAL DU CENTRE by noon today.

2. The 3rd Cav Bde has been ordered to BRAY – the 5th Cav Bde to BINCHE as quickly as possible.

3. Concentrate your Regiment and join remainder of Brigade at BRAY –

4. Send your 'B' Echelon to ESTINNE AU MONT to join remainder.

5. I am moving off for BRAY now via FAUROEULX and ESTINNE AU MONT

6. Acknowledge – Have you got touch with 5th Bde

PEISSANT.
12.5 pm.

R H Keartly May
3 C B.   Brig

MESSAGES AND SIGNALS. "A" Form. Army Form C. 2121.

TO: Preliminary orders & notes.

AAA

1. No sign of Enemy on the front HARVE — MONS. Civilians report hostile Cav. Regt. marching through Roeulx this morning.

2. 3rd Cav Bgde will be responsible for the crossings of the HAINE from PERRONNES exclusive to BOUSSOIT inclusive where it will relieve a post of the 1st Cav Bgde.

3. One squadron 5th Lancers with one Field Troop attached will hold the crossings of above river under special orders given to the Sqn Commander. Reconnaissances being sent to the line HOUDENG – AIMERIES – GOTTIGNIES.

MESSAGES AND SIGNALS.

Army Form C. 2121.

The Bde will probably billet as follows.

Remainder 5th Lancers. BRAY.
Remainder of Bgde about ESTINNE au VAL to which place B Echelon has now been ordered up and billets reconnoitred.

"A" Form.
MESSAGES AND SIGNALS.
Army Form C. 2121

TO { 3rd Bde
Repeated to 2nd Bde.

Sender's Number: P.A.7
Day of Month: 21st
AAA

Have one regiment holding our
from Boussoit to OBOURG. Bde
H.Q. ½ m. S. of BON VOULOIR. Have
seen nothing of enemy

From: 1st Bde
Place:
Time: 1 pm

"A" Form.   Army Form C. 2121.
MESSAGES AND SIGNALS.   No. of Message......

Bray.
Friday. 21. Aug. 14

(2 Field Troop R.E.)

1) Squadron 5 Lancers will hold line of R. Haine from Boussoit (inclusive) to Peronnes (exclusive).

2) Bridges will be placed in a state of defence and all traffic except that of the allied armies will cease between the hours of 8 p.m. and 5.30 a.m.

3) Evening patrols to — (1) Thieu & Gottignies
(2) Strépy - Bracquegnies - Houdeng Aimeries

4) Morning patrols as above & in addition Trivières - La Louvière.
All start at 4 a.m.

5) Report to O.C. 5 Lancers at Bray.
Report your disposition & news as soon as you have reached position assigned.

WHG.
5.b.n.

30

O/o N° 9

3rd Cavalry Brigade Order N° 4
                    BRAY
                    24/8/14

1. It is more than probable that the Cavalry Division will remain in its present position tomorrow.

2. But all units of the Brigade will be ready to saddle up at 4 am, horses then fed.

3. At 6 am the O.C. 4th Hussars will detail 1 Squadron to be at MAURAGE to take over the outposts from the Squadron 5th Lancers.

4. At 6 am the remainder of the Brigade will be in the same position of readiness as it was this afternoon.

5. 'A' Echelon 1st Line Transport will be parked behind the Brigade in its position of readiness.

6. 'B' Echelon 1st Line Transport will move at 6.15 am to ESTINNE AU MONT and Park there. That of 4th Hussars

and the
— Lancers, meeting Brigade
Transport officer at Road junction 1/2
mile west of 13 kilo Stone on main
at 6.15 road to BINCHE, that of 16th Lancers
on joining Commander in ESTINNE AU VAL.

4. Reports tonight to HQrs on main road
just South of BRAY.

Issued at 7.25 pm

H.P. Kearsley Maj
BM
3 C B

"A" Form.
MESSAGES AND SIGNALS.

Army Form C. 2121.
No. of Message: 13a

| Prefix | Code | Words | Charge | This message is on a/c of: | Recd. at | m. |

Office of Origin and Service Instructions.

Sent At ___ m.
To ___
By ___

Service.
(Signature of "Franking Officer.")

Date ___
From ___
By ___

TO 1st, 2nd, 3rd, 4th, 5th Brigades & R.H.A. D.D.M.S.

| Sender's Number | Day of Month | In reply to Number | AAA |
| G(a) 11 | 22/8/14 | | |

The Div will stand fast until it is relieved by the Inf. outpost of the II Corps on the line GIVRY at MONS Canal bridge to NIMY and westward THULIN AAA point north of B line transport echelon 2w GIVRY park concentrate east of This concentration water and feed immediately aaa to be begun Div moves off When the 5th Cav Bde will the Cav. about BINCHE and keep remain with French Cav tonight the and with on its right our II Corps

From Cav. Div.
Place GIVRY.
Time 4.5 a.m.

The above may be forwarded as now corrected. (Z)
Censor. Signature of Addressee or person authorised to telegraph in his name.

* This line should be erased if not required.

"A" Form.
MESSAGES AND SIGNALS.
Army Form C. 2121.

Prefix	Code	m.	Words	Charge		This message is on a/c of:	Recd. at	m.
Office of Origin and Service Instructions.			Sent				Date	
			At		m.	...Service.	From	
			To				By	
			By			(Signature of "Franking Officer.")		

TO 5th D-gs.

Sender's Number	Day of Month	In reply to Number	
BM 17	22		5.10am AAA

Our left flank is holding the bridges at BOUSSOIT in front of your right aaa. One Squadron 4th Hussars is relieving Squadron 5th Lancers there now. aaa. They have been told to get in touch with you aaa GOTTIGNIES and HOUDENG-AIMERIES reported clear this morning.

From 3rd CAV BDE
Place
Time 5.45 am

Signature of Addressor: J.P.H. Causley M.J.

O.C.
  Most Western Regiment
    III Cav. Bde.
      BRAY

I have two troops of 5 D.G's, I Cav. Bde, holding small wood just North of 9 Kilometre Stone between BRAY and VILLERS ST. GHISLAIN. This is the right flank of my brigade.

Please let me know where your left flank is.

  G.H.Herringham
    Captain
    attached 5th D.G's.

All clear here so far.

5.10 am.
22nd August (I think)

"A" Form.
MESSAGES AND SIGNALS.

TO: 3rd C.B.

Sender's Number: PA 27
Day of Month: 22

AAA

Your BM.21 received. 1st Bde. is disposed as yesterday, with E flank at 9th kilometre stone.

Your line appears to be a continuation of our own with right a little forward.

The 5th Lancers refused to take over the defence of Boussoit bridge last night, we had therefore to hold it.

From: 1st C.B.
Place:
Time: 8.45 am

O.C. 5th Lancers Bray. (15)

I have received a telephone message from ROEUX stating that my patrol is there now. I heard on good authority that a German patrol was at the Chateau last night (This information was stamped by La Mairie.)
The 4th Hrs are now sending a patrol R N. of ROEUX

(6.45. am 2d Aug)

MESSAGES AND SIGNALS

LA LOUVIÈRE

To O.C. 5th Lancers

La Louvière all clear.

On arrival I found the bridge here had been barricaded by the enemy reported to have numbered 40-50 but they had retired early this morning.

From reports from intelligent inhabitants I learn that close behind this party were a strong force of the enemy consisting of Uhlans & Hussars, said to number about 1000 men.

The French cavalry are in possession of CARNIÈRES

Inhabitants also report that the enemy have now retired into the territory of ~~Rostin~~ BOIDIN & are holding PONT FAMILLE HEUREUX.

A. G. Carr 2nd Lieut
Officer Patrol A Squadron
5th Lancers

7.15 AM
22.8.14

To. G.O.C.
   3rd Cav. Bde.

My patrol from ROEULX has just returned and reports all clear as far as Mont au BANC just North of ROEULX.
A patrol of 12 German Cavalry passed through ROEULX about 7 a.m and asked their way to HAVRÉ.
An inhabitant states that he saw 4000 Uhlans and Hussars at SOIGNIES yesterday and heard shots in that direction this morning

J. S. Darley Maj
   4⁹ Hussars

To.
OC A Squadron   MAURAGE
     4th Hussars
     22.8.14.

I Reached ROEULX and found all clear.

II A patrol of the enemy 12 men reported to have passed through about 7am and to have asked the road to ~~HAAR~~ HAVRÉ

III I went on to MONT au BANC and an ~~total~~ inhabitant stated that he had seen about 4,000 German cavalry, Uhlans & Hussars at SOIGNIES, yesterday and had heard firing in that direction this morning

             G Greville Lt
                     4th Hussars
             MAURAGE

To O.C. A Sqn.
  4th Hussars

Ref 1/100,000 ② 21 8/14   MAVRAGE
                          10-30 A.M.

I have been through BOIS DU SART
& BOIS DE HAVRE - I was fired
on in BOIS DE HAVE - ~~Instead~~
probably by patrol - I returned
via LES BOIS (E of BOIS DU SART)
through HOUDENG - GOEGNIES
and HOUDENG - AMERIES -
which were clear of Germans
about 10 am.

a Belgian (I saw his passports)
of ~~Fayt~~ - FAYT LES SENEFFE
saw this morning at 8 A.M.

500 Uhlans and 4 Cos. Inf
pass FAYT LES SENEFFE
going towards HAINE STE PIERRE

He had heard of 10,000 G. Inf.
between HAINE STE PIERRE
FAYT LES SENEFFE - JOLIMENT

Mataire Capt
4th Hussars

Copy No. 3

OPERATION ORDER No. 2
by
Major General E.H.H. ALLENBY, C.B., Commanding Cavalry Division.

22nd Aug. 1914.

1. (a) No further information about the enemy.
   (b) The 2nd Army is holding the line GIVRY - MONS - THULIN.
   The 5th Cavalry Brigade is no longer under the orders of the G.O.C. Cavalry Division.

2. The Division will move into the area THULIN - QUIEVRAIN - AUDREGNIES - ELOUGES.

3. (a) Right Column.
   Starting point, cross roads about one third of a mile due north of the R in HARVENG. Time, 12 noon. Route, MALADRIE - south of Point 895 CIPLY - road and railway crossing one mile north of the F in FRANERIES - WASMES - BOIS-de-BOUSSU.
   4th Cavalry Brigade, 7th Bde.R.H.A., 2nd Cavalry Brigade, 1st Cavalry Brigade, Signal Squadron, Field Squadron.
   (b) Centre Column.
   Starting point, western exit of GIVRY; 12 noon. Route, PATURAGES - DOUR. Composition, 7th R.H.A.Bde. Amm.Col.
   (c) 3rd Cavalry Brigade and 3rd Bde R.H.A. will move under special instructions.

4. "B" Echelon 1st line transport and 3rd Bde.R.H.A. Amm Col. will leave cross roads south east of GIVRY at 12 noon. Route, GOGNIES - BLAREGNIES - SARS-la-BRUYERE - BLAUGIES - to WIHERIES where the head will halt.

5. Billeting areas are allotted as follows :-
   1st Cav.Bde. ... AUDREGNIES.
   2nd Cav.Bde. ... THULIN.
   3rd Cav.Bde. ... ELOUGES.
   4th Cav.Bde. ... QUIEVERAIN.
   H.Q. & Div.Troops QUIEVERAIN.

6. Reports to the head of the Column.

J. VAUGHAN. Colonel. G.S.

Issued at 9.45 a.m.

Received.
11 am.

"A" Form. Army Form C. 2121.
MESSAGES AND SIGNALS. No. of Message _____

Prefix	Code	m.	Words	Charge	This message is on a/c of:	Recd. at		m.
Office of Origin and Service Instructions.			Sent		Service.	Date	(16)	
			At	m.		From		
			To		(Signature of "Franking Officer.")	By		
			By					

TO | 5th | Cav | Bde |
      | | near BINCHE | |

Sender's Number.	Day of Month	In reply to Number		AAA
BM.27	22			

have	been	ordered	to	fall
back	to	ridge	between	10
and	9	kilo	stone	just
west	of	BRAY	and	then
~~left behind~~		just	Brigade	aaa
General	Allenby	asks	me	to
order	you	to	retire	slowly
through	ESTINNE	AU VAL	and	get
in	touch	with	the	Right
of	1st	Brigade	near	9
kilo	stone	just	west	of
BRAY	aaa.	I	will	stay
about	BRAY	to	cover	your
retreat.				

From	3rd Cav Bde			
Place	½ north of BRAY			
Time	1·15 pm			

The above may be forwarded as now corrected.   (Z) R M Crawley Major.
Censor. Signature of Addressor or person authorised to telegraph in his name.
* This line should be erased if not required.

				Sch. 4a.	"A" Form.			Army Form C. 2121.
				MESSAGES AND SIGNALS.		No. of Message		

Prefix	Code	m.	Words	Charge	This message is on a/c of:	Recd. at 17 m.
Office of Origin and Service Instructions.						Date
			Sent		Service.	From
			At m.			
			To			
			By		(Signature of "Franking Officer.")	By

TO 1st 2nd 3rd 4th Cav. Bdes.

Sender's Number	Day of Month	In reply to Number	
G(a)19	22nd		AAA

The withdrawal of the Division will commence at 5 p.m. in the following order aaa 3rd Bde via HARMIGNIES and HARVENG to the GIVRY – PATURAGES road aaa the 1st Bde via HARMIGNIES and HARVENG and follow the 3rd Bde aaa the 4th Bde from HALTE to 9th kilo stone GIVRY – MONS road and HARVENG to follow the 1st Bde aaa the 2nd Bde will cover this movement holding the hill N. of HARMIGNIES and march with a small rearguard aaa from PATURAGES bdes can march to their cantonments by the most convenient routes

From Cav Div
Place HALTE near VELLEREILLES-LE-SEC
Time 4.30 pm

(Z) T. Vaughan. Col

MESSAGES AND SIGNALS.

Army Form C. 2121.

Prefix	Code	m.	Words	Charge	This message is on a/c of:	Recd. at ... m.
Office of Origin and Service Instructions.			Sent		Service.	Date ...
			At ... m.			From ...
			To		(Signature of "Franking Officer.")	By
			By			

TO 1st Hussars

Sender's Number 29 Day of Month 22 In reply to Number   A A A

Call in all your posts preparatory to the retirement of the Brigade on ELOUGES via VILLERS ST GHISLAIN and HARMIGNIES aaa. Major MacTaggart has been ordered to retire immediately on us here. aaa. You will receive further orders when to move. aaa. Please inform Boys on Eicer near BUSSOIT that you are about to retire.

From 3rd Cav Bde
Place 9 Kilo BRAY
Time 4.55 pm

R H Rawley Maj

(Z)

Censor.   Signature of Addressor or person authorised to telegraph in his name.

* This line should be erased if not required.

Omaha order No 3

1. The Cav Div + the 19th Inf Bde will tie back South West tomorrow morning as under

Route A	Route B	Route C
WARGNIES	IONLAIN	West of Route B
VILLERS POL	MARESCHES	of Route B
RUESNES	SEMERIES	
VERTAIN	BERMERAIN	
	HAUSSY	

Units allotted to route A, the 1st Troops now bivouac'y at WARGNIES (other than cav units) under the command of Col O Reat KHA

The 19th Inf Bde + the 4th Cav Bde are allotted route B
The 1st + 2nd Cav Bdes + pk Bn, gen. C.F. Briggs who forms the rear guard of the 2nd Corps + the Cav Div.

The 4th and 3rd Cav Bdes L under & J Batt RHA
Maj Gen Allenby will form the
flank guard.

The tail of the transport & amm
columns must be clear of the LE
QUESNOY – MAING railway by
5.30 am and the tail of the
fighting troops with the exception
of the rear guard must be clear
of the line WARGNIES LE GRAND –
CURGIES by 6am
The 1st bound of the rear guard
will be to the line FRASNOY –
PRESEAU.

J Vaughan Col

"A" Form.
MESSAGES AND SIGNALS.
Army Form C. 2121.

| TO | 3rd No 5. | Cavalry Brigade HOMBLIERES | Order 27/8/14. |

AAA

1. Our 1st Army is retiring in good order approximately via GUISE on RIBEMONT. All transport having got quietly away. But there is a mass of fugitives of the Second Army on line ST QUENTIN — PÉRONNE

2. The 3rd Cav Bde and attached troops will move at once to ST QUENTIN to feed the men and horses, and afterwards moving in a northerly direction to assist in covering the retirement of the 2nd army.

3. The 4th Hussars will move at once to HARLY (NW) halting at the junction of the GUISE—ST QUENTIN — MESNIL HARLY Roads. The 3rd Bde RHA will remain in their present position to cover the retirement of the remainder

MESSAGES AND SIGNALS.

of	the	Brigade	through	HOMBLIERES
and	then	will	move	along
main	GUISE	- ST QUENTIN	road.	

4. The remainder of the Brigade will march in the following order through HOMBLIERES and along the GUISE - ST QUENTIN road.

      Composite Regt
      5th Lancers
      16th Lancers (less 2 troops)
Rear 2 troops 16th Lancers.

5. Reports to the head of the Composite Regiment.

Issued 8.30 am   R.H. Keartley Major
                                3 C.B.

MESSAGES AND SIGNALS.

Army Form C. 2121.

TO 3rd Cav. Bde.   Operation Order No 6
HARLY
27/8/14

(1) The 4th Corps billets tonight about MONT D'ORIGNY
The Second Corps is now moving between ST QUENTIN and MAY
The 1st Corps is billets tonight about GRUGIES

(2) The 3rd Cav Bde and 3rd Bde RHA will billet as follows:—
(a) H.Q.s & 16th Lancers (less 1 sqn) MESNIL
(b) 1 Sqn 16th Lancers HOMBLIERES
(c) 5th Lancers NEUVILLE
(d) 4th Hussars & 3rd Bde RHA ITANCOURT
(e) party hall moon at once under the orders of Col. Pitcairn.
(a)(b)(c) will move as soon as the men have had their teas
(d) as soon as the remainder have gone.

MESSAGES AND SIGNALS.

All parties will send on their billeting parties at once.

3. O.C. billeting areas will carry out the duties of their billets.

The squadron at HOMBLIERES under special instructions issued (verbally) to O.C. 16ᵗʰ Lancers.

4. Reports to MESNIL after 3 p.m.

5. Unless further orders are issued the Brigade will not leave billets before 6 a.m.

Signed at 2 p.m.

R.H. Kearsley Major
   Bᵈᵉ M.

365

"A" Form.   Army Form C. 2121.
MESSAGES AND SIGNALS.

Prefix	Code	m.	Words	Charge	This message is on a/c of:	Recd. at	m.
Office of Origin and Service Instructions.			Sent			Date	
			At	m.	Service.	From	
			To			By	
			By		(Signature of "Franking Officer.")		

TO   2nd Cav. Bgde.

Sender's Number.	Day of Month	In reply to Number	
* G.7.W. 21.	27		AAA

Second Corps Commdr. has assumed command of all troops in the vicinity, including those of the Cavalry Div. AAA. He understands that you are out of touch with the rest of the Division AAA. You will therefore until further orders act on the following instructions and if in the course of carrying them out you come in touch with Gen Allenby, or with any other detached portion of the Div: you will give information of these instructions to the Commanders and will inform them that they apply equally to their own commands.

Your first duty is the protection of the rear of the corps (and especially of the 5th Div. Retiring by the MAURETZ – St QUENTIN – OLLEZY road)

From		
Place		
Time		

The above may be forwarded as now corrected.   (Z)

Censor.   Signature of Addresser or person authorised to telegraph in his name.
* This line should be erased if not required.

Wt. W1154/2240. 7/11. 7,500,000. Sch. 4a. "A" Form.   Army Form C. 2121.

MESSAGES AND SIGNALS.

Prefix......Code......m	Words	Charge	This message is on a/c of:	Recd. at.........m.
Office of Origin and Service Instructions.	Sent		..................Service.	Date..............
....	At..........m.			From.............
....	To..........			
....	By..........		(Signature of "Franking Officer.")	By..............

TO			
Sender's Number.	Day of Month	In reply to Number	

*   AAA

The corps will endeavour finally to reorganise behind the line of the SOMBRE canal between OLLEZY and OFFOY AAA. It may not reach that line until the 29 inst. or even later.

Your second mission is to give the corps Comdr. information as to the state of affairs in rear of the Corps (and especially in rear of the 1st Divn Commanr.)

   a. Is there any formed infantry rearguard?
   b. Has the rearguard got guns
   c. Position of rearguard of column at various times.
   D. Any abandoned transport and guns.
   e. So far as possible state of organisation of divisions.

From			S Forestier Walker
Place			B.S.
Time			1 Corps

The above may be forwarded as now corrected.   (Z)

....
Censor.   Signature of Addressee or person authorised to telegraph in his name.

* This line should be erased if not required.

Wt. W. 1/2240. 7/11. 7,500,000. Sch. 4a. "A" Form   Army Form C. 2121.
MESSAGES AND SIGNALS.

Prefix	Code	In Words	Charge	This message is on a/c of:	Recd. at	m.
Office of Origin and Service Instructions.		Sent			Date	
		At	m.	Service.	From	
		To				
		By		(Signature of "Franking Officer.")	By	

TO ARMY Hd Qrs NOYON.

Sender's Number	Day of Month	In reply to Number		AAA
BM4.	28			

My	present	position	is	Watching
the	line	ESSIGNY	– CERIZY	aaa
My	object	to	cover	the
gap	between	1st	and	2nd
Armies	aaa.	I	have	received
no	orders	for	four	days
from	anyone	please	send	me
definite	orders	with	① the	intention
of	the	army	② my	role
in	this	plan.	aaa	
have lost touch with			Cavalry	Divisional
Headquarters and	all	the	3rd Bde	Brigade R.H.A.
Baggage aaa	The			
is	with	me	and	has
lost	touch	with	its	ammunition
Column	and	baggage	aaa	we
are	dangerously short	of	ball	and

From
Place
Time

The above may be forwarded as now corrected.   (Z)

Censor.   Signature of Addresser or person authorised to telegraph in his name.
* This line should be erased if not required.

MESSAGES AND SIGNALS.   "A" Form.   Army Form C. 2121.

Shell ammunition and must have supplies this afternoon, also all artillery and Cavalry here. aaa. We also want to know where we can evacuate horses and dismounted men and obtain remounts and equipment. aaa Send an iron ration with supply column and preserved meat instead of fish meat for immediate consumption. aaa. My present intention is to billet in REMIGNY this afternoon please send supply column there also maps at we have none of this district in this brigade.

From: 3rd CAV BDE
Place: ESSIGNY LE GRAND
Time: 11.40 am

R. H. Kearsley May 18th

"A" Form.
MESSAGES AND SIGNALS.
Army Form C. 2121

Prefix	Code	m.	Words	Charge		This message is on a/c of:	Recd. at	m.
Office of Origin and Service Instructions.			Sent			Keep	Date	
			At	m.		Service.	From	
			To				By	
			By			(Signature of "Franking Officer.")		

TO 3rd CAV BDE ORDER No 9
[illegible] between PAILLOUET and FRIERES
[illegible]

Sender's Number	Day of Month	In reply to Number	AAA

1. The Brigade and attached troops will billet tonight as follows:—
   No 1 Squad Regt — [illegible] N of FRIERES
   3rd RHA — [illegible] — FRIERES
   4th Hussars — PAILLOUET
   16th Lancers — JUSSY

2. [illegible paragraph about patrols, bridge at MENNESSIS, communication with 1st Army Corps at HAM, Monte Stampé, sending out patrols in the morning as directed by the GOC]

3. [illegible paragraph about billets, ammunition, billets being made as possible, animals to be fed and cared for]

4. [illegible] Army advances tomorrow the Brigade will move at 7am to the [illegible]

From
Place
Time

The above may be forwarded as now corrected. (Z)
Censor.   Signature of Addressor or person authorised to telegraph in his name
* This line should be erased if not required.

"A" Form.   Army Form C. 2121
MESSAGES AND SIGNALS.   No. of Message_____

Prefix_____ Code_____m.	Words	Charge	This message is on a/c of:	Recd. at_____m.
	Sent			Date_____
Office of Origin and Service Instructions.	At_____m.		_____Service.	From_____
	To_____			By_____
	By_____		(Signature of "Franking Officer.")	

TO {

| * | Sender's Number | Day of Month | In reply to Number | A A A |

	the	Brigade	will	remain	in
	its	present	billets	tomorrow.	
5.	An officer has been sent into General
	Headquarters to enquire about — Supplies —
	Ammunition (Ball & shell) — the evacuation
	of sick horses and dismounted men — the
	supply of Remounts — horse shoes — etc. maps
	Sunday 6.15 pm		R.N. Kearsley Major
			3 C.B.
	Our first army billets tonight about LA FERE
	will outposts on the line VENDEUIL — LIEZ.

From	
Place	
Time	

The above may be forwarded as now corrected. (Z)

Censor. Signature of Addressee or person authorised to telegraph in his name
* This line should be erased if not required.

"A" Form.
MESSAGES AND SIGNALS.
Army Form C. 2121

Prefix......Code......m.	Words	Charge			
Office of Origin and Service Instructions.			This message is on a/c of:	Recd. at..........m.	
	Sent			Date..........	
	At..........m.		..........Service.	From..........	
	To..........			By..........	
	By..........		(Signature of "Franking Officer.")		

TO 3rd Cav. Bgde

Sender's Number	Day of Month	In reply to Number	
* G. 188	Twenty-ninth		AAA

Ref ce your report of hostile (Columns) moving towards ESSIGNY and VENDEUIL AAA 5th Cav Brigade had a very successful fight with Guard Uhlans at north of CERIZY yesterday afternoon AAA I do not intend to make any movement tomorrow as my troops require rest When I move it will be with my whole force united AAA the position of my troops is shown on the accompanying sketch map. You will remain in observation in your present position and if pressed fall

From 1st Corps
Place
Time

The above may be forwarded as now corrected.

(Z) M Malcolm Vde

Censor.   Signature of Addressee or person authorised to telegraph in his name

* This line should be erased if not required.

"A" Form.
MESSAGES AND SIGNALS.
Army Form C. 212

TO: Pap ?

back upon CHAUNY and be responsible for holding the bridges at CHAUNY and SENICOURT — The 5th Cavalry Brigade will be at SINCENY to-day and will be responsible for the VIRY bridge —

Have you sufficient dispatch riders to enable you to keep touch with me — AAA and sending two with this message for you to keep if required.

From: 1st Caps
Place:
Time: 5. 50 am

"C" Form (Original). Army Form C. 2123.
MESSAGES AND SIGNALS. No. of Message _____

Prefix	Code	Words	Received	Sent, or sent out	Office Stamp.
		£ s. d.	From 27	At ___ m.	
Charges to collect			By wire	To ___	
Service Instructions.				By ___	

Handed in at the GHQ Office, at 12·35 m. Received here at 2.20 m.

TO Cav Div and 2nd Cav Bde

Sender's Number.	Day of Month.	In reply to Number.	AAA
OA 360	29th Aug		

2nd	Cav	Bde	at
GOLANCOURT	is	engaged	with
what	is	probably	one
hostile	division	advancing	from
HAM	aaa	move	in
support	aaa	The	French
are	advancing	on	St-QUENTIN
from	the	south	east
against	the	left	rear
of	the	enemy	acknowledge

FROM GHQ 1235
PLACE
TIME

*This line should be erased if not required.

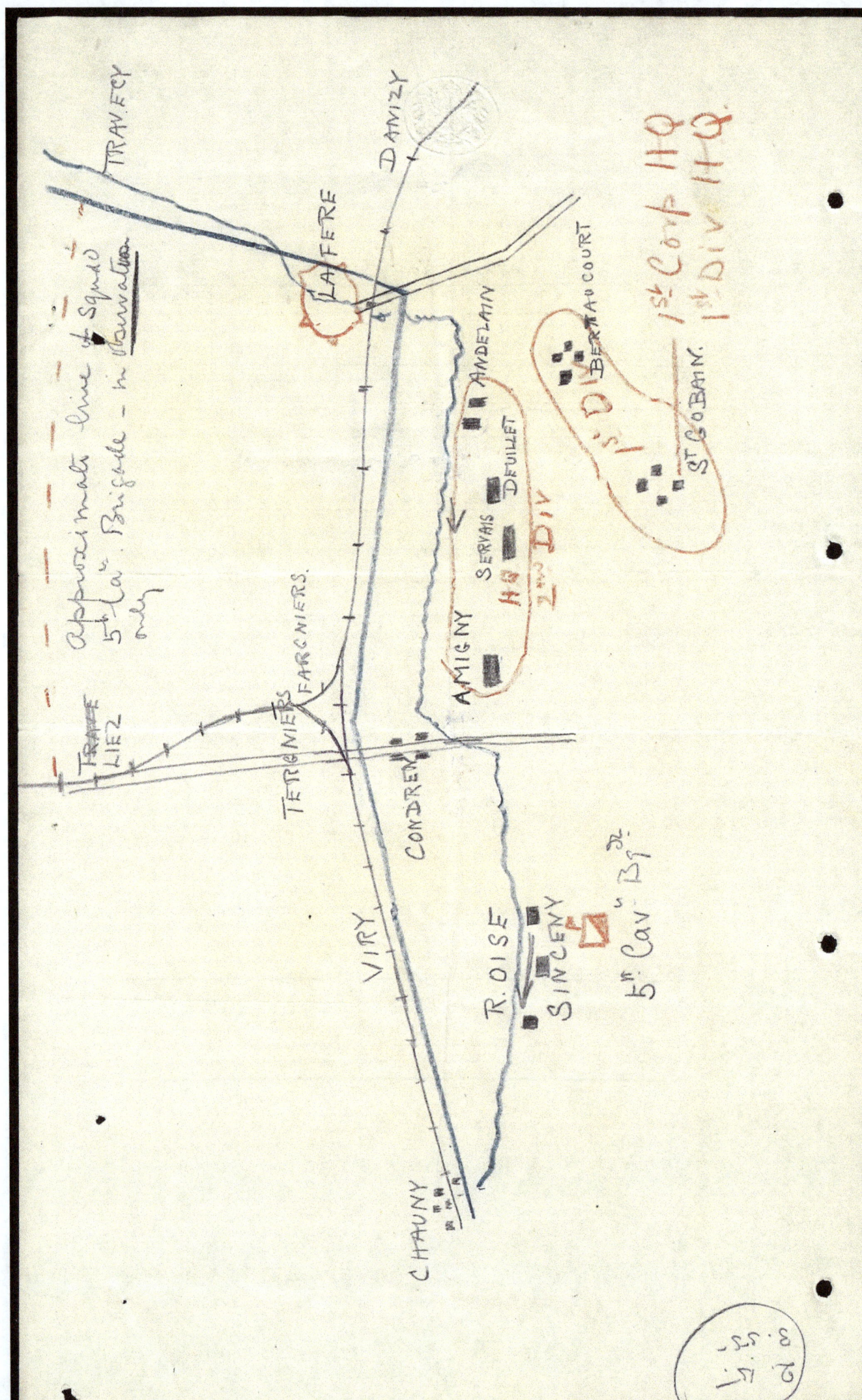

Wt. W1154/2240. 7/11. 7,500,000. Sch. 4a. "A" Form.					Army Form C. 2121.
MESSAGES AND SIGNALS.					No. of Message_____
Prefix____ Code____ m.	Words	Charge	This message is on a/c of:		Recd. at_____ m.
Office of Origin and Service Instructions.					Date_____
_____	Sent		_____		From_____
_____	At____ m.		_____Service.		
_____	To____		_____		
_____	By____		(Signature of "Franking Officer.")		By_____

TO G ~~1st Divt 3rd N. Cavalry Brigade~~
     HQrs   3rd Cav Bde

Sender's Number.	Day of Month	In reply to Number	AAA
* GL.29	Twenty-ninth		

Owing to allies having suffered a reverse it is necessary for the 1st Corps to fall back AAA. All troops must be withdrawn south of river ~~at~~ except light patrols ~~even~~ AAA Bridges to be blown up at 3 am AAA. Transport ~~has~~ already started Troops move 3.30 am as follows 1st Division ~~but~~ if all quiet but if there is any danger of their being rushed they will be
X destroyed at once AAA. Transport started 9 p.m. Troops will move as follows behind R. Aisne
   1st Division by roads allotted to transport as far as LAFFAUX thence via SOISSONS to ~~REIMS~~

From
Place X. patrols will of course   MISSY aux Bois
Time   be withdrawn

The above may be forwarded as now corrected.   (Z)

Censor.   Signature of Addresser or person authorised to telegraph in his name.
* This line should be erased if not required.

Handwriting
Neil Malcolm
I Corps

MESSAGES AND SIGNALS.

Wt. W1154/2240. 7/11. 7,500,000. Sch. 4a. "A" Form. Army Form C. 2121.

to p.p. eastward of town
2nd Division

Keeping on east side of SOISSONS
AAA 2nd Division from by
TERNY west side of SOISSONS
to PERNANT
Cavalry
5th Brigade to cover the
rear and eastern flank
of the Corps and retire through
SOISSONS by road allotted to
1st Division.
3rd Brigade to cover the western
flank and to connect with
2nd Corps whilst retiring to the
west of FONTENOY. will cross the AISNE at
FONTENOY. The 3rd Cav Bde

Wt. W1154/2240. 7/11. 7,500,000. Sch. 4a.	"A" Form.			Army Form C. 2121.
	MESSAGES AND SIGNALS.			No. of Message

Prefix	Code	m.	Words	Charge	This message is on a/c of:	Recd. at	m.
Office of Origin and Service Instructions.			Sent			Date	
			At	m.	Service.	From	
			To				
			By		(Signature of "Franking Officer.")	By	

TO —

| Sender's Number. | Day of Month | In reply to Number | AAA |

2nd ~~Division~~

Obstructions must be made to block the roads in rear of the troops as they retire — and * bridges destroyed when possible. AAA. Report to TERNY 5 miles N of SOISSONS after 5 am AAA. Report progress ~~~~ of columns across the CANAL de L'OISE et AISNE

All heavy impedimenta such as pontoon wagons etc must be sent well ahead of troops

From   * This refers to bridges other
Place   than those over OISE already
Time   prepared

The above may be forwarded as now corrected. (Z)

Censor.   Signature of Addressee or person authorised to telegraph in his na

* This line should be erased if not required.

Army Form C. 2121.

"A" Form.

No. of Message

MESSAGES AND SIGNALS.

Prefix ... Code ... m.	Words	Charge	This message is on a/c of:	Recd. at ... m.
Office of Origin and Service Instructions.	Sent		... Service.	Date
	At ... m.			From
	To		(Signature of "Franking Officer.")	By
	By			

TO { 4th Hussars (?) / 5th Lancers / 3rd Bde RHA (?) | Amm Col / Fd Amb

Sender's Number	Day of Month	In reply to Number	AAA
* BM 10.	21 (?)		

All previous orders [illegible] have been cancelled and [illegible] [illegible] [illegible] at [illegible] [illegible] [illegible] all [illegible] [illegible] [illegible] [illegible] commencing at 9 am this morning [illegible] [illegible] billet as follows

4th Hussars [illegible] at [illegible] [illegible] [illegible] [illegible] [illegible] RETHEUIL (?) with 2 troops at RETHEUIL (?)

5th Lancers MORTFONTAINE

3rd Bde RHA between ROYE (?) and TILLEUL (?)

Amm Col } TAILLEFONTAINE
Field Amb }

Bde HQrs ROY ST NICHOLAS

All units will be ready to move at 4 am.

From 3 CB (?)

Place

Time 8.30 am (?)

The above may be forwarded as now corrected.

Censor.

(Z) [illegible signature] Maj (?) 1914 (?)

Signature of Addressor or person authorised to telegraph in his name.

* This line should be erased if not required.

Wt. W1154/2240. 7/11. 7,500,000. Sch. 4a. "A" Form. Army Form C. 2121.

MESSAGES AND SIGNALS.

No. of Message_____

Prefix____ Code____ m. | Words | Charge | This message is on a/c of: | Recd. at _____ m.
Office of Origin and Service Instructions. | Sent | | _____Service. | Date_____
_____ | At____ m. | | | From_____
_____ | To____ | | |
 | By | | (Signature of "Franking Officer.") | By

TO 5th Cav. Bde. order No 8
    PIERRE MANDE
    30/9/14

Sender's Number. | Day of Month | In reply to Number | A A A

1. G... armies bivouac tonight behind R. MISNE — They just enemy through Soissons. Its left division along the road BUCY SIS — ROZEMBRAY — TERNY — west of SOISSONS — PERNAN.

2. ... task allotted to the 5th Cav. Bde. is to protect the west flank of the 1st Army.

3. I consigned the Room 16th Lancers Gd immediately under Major ROTHERVILLE — BICKARD AT — MINICAMP. Remainder of the Brigade will move at 3.30 am in the following order starting from the cross roads in PIERREMONDE. 5th Lancers — 8th Hussars — 4th Division R.H.A. — ISAC D'ARBLINCOURT — S. PAUL — ST AUBIN — MORSAIN — NOUVRON — FONTENOY

From | | |
Place | | |
Time | | |
The above may be forwarded as now corrected. (Z)
....
Censor. Signature of Addresser or person authorised to telegraph in his name.
* This line should be erased if not required.

Wt. W1154/2240. 7/11. 7,500,000. Sch. 4a. "A" Form. Army Form C. 2121.

MESSAGES AND SIGNALS.

No. of Message

Prefix .... Code .... m. | Words | Charge

Office of Origin and Service Instructions.

Sent
At .... m.
To ....
By ....

This message is on a/c of:
.... *Service.*
(Signature of "Franking Officer.")

Recd. at .... m.
Date ....
From ....
By ....

TO

Sender's Number.	Day of Month	In reply to Number	AAA
*			

When this column reaches [illegible]
the 16 Lancers will become Rearguard,
when they will keep a look out
on the following road along which are
[illegible] – PIERREMONDE –
[illegible] – [illegible] – LA [illegible]
– [illegible] – [illegible] – [illegible]
[illegible]

4. Report to main body at [illegible].

Issued at 2 am.

[illegible signature]

From
Place
Time

The above may be forwarded as now corrected. (Z)

Censor. Signature of Addressor or person authorised to telegraph in his name.

* This line should be erased if not required.

"A" Form.   Army Form C. 2121.

MESSAGES AND SIGNALS.

Prefix	Code	m.	Words	Charge	This message is on a/c of:	Recd. at	m.
Office of Origin and Service Instructions.			Sent			Date	
copy			At	m.	Service.	From	
			To				
			By		(Signature of "Franking Officer.")	By	

TO	1st Division		5th Cavalry Bde
	2nd Division		
	3rd Cavalry Bde		

Sender's Number.	Day of Month	In reply to Number	
Gc.33	30th		AAA

Troops will halt for two hours after
crossing the CANAL de L'OISE et AISNE aaa
Bridge will be held ~~it~~ as follows with
infantry and mounted troops
    1st Division AIZY to VAUXAILLON
    2nd Division PONT-A-COURZON - CRECY-AU-
       MONT
    5th Cavalry Bde continue to right
    3rd Cavalry Bde continue to left
Troops will not cross the AISNE today
Billetting area are allotted as
follows:-
    5th Cavalry Bde JOUY - AIZY - BAILLY
    1st Division MARGAVAL - VUILLERY
BRAYE - CROUY - BUCI - LE LONG
    2nd Division CIAMECY - CHAIVIGNY -
CUFFIES - PASLY - POMIERS

P.T.O

The above may be forwarded as now corrected.   (Z)

Censor.   Signature of Addressor or person authorised to telegraph in his name.

* This line should be erased if not required.

Wt. W1154/2240. 7/11. 7,500,000. Sch. 4a. "A" Form. Army Form...

MESSAGES AND SIGNALS.

No. of Message_____

Prefix _____ Code _____ m.	Words	Charge	This message is on a/c of:	Recd. at _____ m.
Office of Origin and Service Instructions.	Sent			Date _____
_____	At _____ m.		_____ Service.	From _____
_____	To _____		(Signature of "Franking Officer.")	By _____
	By _____			

TO

| Sender's Number. | Day of Month | In reply to Number | |
| G.C.33 | | | AAA |

3rd Cavalry Brigade NOUVRON-FONTENOI
1st Army HQ CHAU____ S.E. of second
U in VAUXBUIN

Only such portions of the train of the 1st
and 2nd Divisions as is absolutely
necessary in each case should be
retained in billetting areas the
remainder should be passed through
SOISSONS and parked W. of the SOISSONS-
PARIS Road Second Division opposite
VAUXBUIN First Division one mile
further South

From 1st Corps
Place
Time 7.25 am

The above may be forwarded as now corrected.   (Z) (Sd) J. Gough.

Censor. Signature of Addressor or person authorised to telegraph in his name.
* This line should be erased if not required.

"A" Form.
MESSAGES AND SIGNALS.

Army Form C. 2121.

Prefix	Code	Words	Charge	This message is on a/c of:	Recd. at	m.
Office of Origin and Service Instructions.		Sent		Service.	Date	
		At	m.		From	
		To			By	
		By		(Signature of "Franking Officer.")		

TO 3rd Cav Bde

Sender's Number	Day of Month	In reply to Number	AAA
G-105			

I	am	uncertain	whether	yr
get	Cav	Div	orders	of
29th	sent	to	as	afsn
he	a	victor	can	15 A A
It	is	very	important	that
you	should	get	to	RETHONDES
this	afternoon	so	that	we
can	send	your	to	A
echelon	Sqn	15th	2	and
other	details	to	yr	3d
to	A	echelon	as	this
could		consul	be	put
from	RETHONDES	to-day	AAA	1/4
this	relief	last	night	of
NAMPCEL	A	from	the	IV 20.
Cav	line	to	march	on
Schenkwick	Tracy	AAA	5	our

From
Place
Time

The above may be forwarded as now corrected. (Z)

Censor. Signature of Addressor or person authorised to telegraph in his name.

* This line should be erased if not required.

"A" Form.   Army Form C. 2121.
                    MESSAGES AND SIGNALS.   No. of Message

Prefix	Code	m.	Words	Charge	Office of Origin and Service Instructions.		This message is on a/c of:	Recd. at m.
			Sent				Service.	Date
			At	m.				From
			To					By
			By		(Signature of "Franking Officer.")			

TO

Sender's Number	Day of Month	In reply to Number		AAA
G-105				
You	at	G.H.Q.	Compiegne	and
have	been	told	that	1st
Corps	will	halt	at	COUCY
le	CHATEAU	and	the	IInd
Corps	about	BLERANCOURDELL		AAA
Think	you	can	easily	join
between	these	two	and	work
on	the	latter	to	BETHONDES
AAA	Try	and	get	in
as	early	as	possible	as
time	is	a	bit	of
moving	out	to	do	AAA
You	can	evacuate	sick	oil
horses	here	and	may	get
remounts	in	two	days	AAA
Our	H.Q.	on	at	Railway
Station				

From CAV DIV
Place COMPIEGNE
Time 7-45

The above may be forwarded as now corrected.   (Z)   J Vaughan

                Censor.   Signature of Addressor or person authorised to telegraph in
* This line should be erased if not required.

"A" Form.
MESSAGES AND SIGNALS.
Army Form C. 2121

Prefix .... Code .... in.	Words	Charge	This message is on a/c of:	Recd. at .... m.
Office of Origin and Service Instructions.	Sent			Date ....
	At .... m.		Service.	From ....
	To			By ....
	By		(Signature of "Franking Officer.")	

TO { 1st Division   5th Cavalry Bde
     2nd Division
     3rd Cavalry Bde

| Sender's Number | Day of Month | In reply to Number | AAA |
| G.215 | 30th | | |

GHQ report that situation appears still better this morning retirement will therefore be stopped and troops will halt until one pm in the positions ordered in my G.c 33 aaa 5th Cavalry Brigade will keep touch with French left at La Fere and push patrols towards River OISE west of that place aaa 3rd Cavalry Brigade will conform Report to TERNY position of your HQ and what bridges if any have been destroyed

From 1st Corps
Place TERNY
Time 9.50 am

OPERATION ORDER No.3
by
Major-General E.H.H. ALLENBY, C.B., Commanding Cavalry Division.

Copy No. 4

29th August 1914.

1. (a). Two hostile columns were located to-day with their heads at GUISCARD and NESLE.

   (b). The Cavalry Division is in touch with our 2nd Army at NOYON and French forces at ROYE.

   (c). The 5th Cavalry Brigade is attached to the 1st Army: the 2nd Cavalry Brigade to the 2nd Army.

2. The Cavalry Division will concentrate about COMPIEGNE.

3. In consequence the following movements will take place.

   (a) All transport about LASSIGNY will move under command of Colonel Thring via ELINCOURT and COUDUN and park near the railway station at the cross roads west of COMPIEGNE.

   (b) 4th Cavalry Brigade, Ansell's detachment, H.Q. Cav.Div., R.H.A. and Signal Squadron will march via THIESCOURT to the I of ECOUVILLON, RIBECOURT to CLAIROIX. Starting point, point 91 south of DIVETTE: time, six a.m.; Order of march, Signal Squadron, Div.H.Q., Ansell's detachment. I. Battery R.H.A., 4th Cavalry Brigade (less one regiment), and one section R.H.A. to be detailed as rear guard.

   (c) The 1st Cavalry Brigade will march from BAILLY to CHOISY-au-BAC, arriving there by 12 noon.

   (d) The 3rd Cavalry Brigade will march to NAMPCELL, and off saddle. So soon as the 2nd Corps is clear he will resume his march and billet at RETHONDES.

   (e) All other units of the Division whether of fighting troops or administrative units, will march to the railway station at COMPIEGNES.

4. During the afternoon all the transport of Brigades will march to join their respective units.

5. Reports to DIVES until seven a.m. After that hour to the railway station at COMPIEGNE.

Issued at 10.35 p.m.

J. VAUGHAN. Colonel. G.S.

OPERATION ORDER No.4   Copy No. 2
by
Major General E.H.H. ALLENBY C.B., Commanding Cavalry Division.

30th August 1914.

1. (a). Yesterday the 2nd Corps was attacked south of HAM by the VII German Corps which had advanced from ST. QUENTIN that morning, but which met with but little success. The pressure, such as it was, was relieved by a French advance in force on our right which met with great success in the neighbourhood of GUISE, where the German Guard and X Corps were driven back into the OISE. On our left French forces were engaged with the enemy in the direction of PERONNE, but the action was not pressed by the Germans, who had slightly withdrawn during the early hours of the afternoon.

   (b). The Army will move West to-morrow.

2. The Cavalry Division will cover the movement on the north bank of the OISE.

3. Divisional assembly point - the valley half mile south west of the "d" in ROUTE d'AMIENS.

   The 4th Brigade will cover the assembly with one regiment getting touch with the 3rd Hussars at COUDUN and watching to the south west as far as the railway two miles west of VENETTE and reconnoitring ANTHUIL - MONCHY and MONT MARTIN. The 4th Brigade will complete its assembly by 6.30 a.m.; the 1st Brigade by 7 a.m.

   They will march via the main bridge near the railway station to VENETTE thence north up the valley.

   The R.H.A. will accompany the Brigades to which they are attached.
   The 3rd Brigade will march west in rear of the II Corps crossing the river at PORT de la CROIX ST OUEN, and billet at RIVECOURT, where it will be joined by its 1st line transport and details.

   The Transport will march in the following order under Colonel Thring, starting at 8 a.m. - Signal Squadron, Field Squadron R.E., Ammunition Columns, Field Ambulances, Divisional Headquarters, 1st line transport in order, 4th, 1st and 3rd Brigades. This column will assemble in a concealed position west of the main road ready to cross the PORT de la CROIX ST OUEN at 10 a.m. The Signal Squadron will erect a wireless station and establish an Intelligence centre near this point.

4. Billeting areas :-
   1st Brigade - SARRON.   3rd Brigade - RIVECOURT.
   4th Brigade - BAZICOURT.
   Divisional H.Q. and Divisional Troops - PLESSIS VILLETTE.

5. Reports to Divisional Headquarters, HOTEL de la CLOCHE till 6.30 a.m., After that hour to Divisional Assembly point.

         Issued at 8.30 p.m.   J. VAUGHAN. Colonel. G.S.

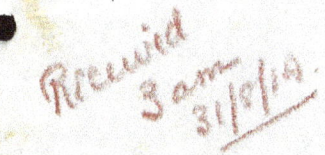
Received 3am 31/8/14

3rd Cav Bde

Copy No. 7

1st ARMY CORPS OPERATION ORDER No. 4.

30th August, 1914.

(1). Our Allies engaged the enemy successfully north of GUISE yesterday and inflicted great loss upon him. A French reserve corps is now in the billets vacated by us this morning. The 5th French Corps is to the east of us, and our 2nd Corps to the west.

(2) The march will be continued tomorrow in a south-westerly direction.

    1st Division by CROUY and SOISSONS to area VAUX BUIN - SACONIN-BREUIL - MISSY-AUX-BOIS.

    2nd Division will cross the River AISNE at POMMIERES to area PERNANT - LAVERSINE - CUTRY - COEUVRES et VALSERY. Bridge to be clear for cavalry by 11 a.m.

    Cavalry to cover retirement, cross at POMMIERES after 11 a.m. and billet in area DOMMIERES - ST. PIERRE - AIGLE.

    1st and 2nd Division Ammunition Columns to VILLERS COTTERET.

(3) Rendezvous at railhead. Times will be notified direct to formations.

(4) Reports to CHATEAU, ½ mile east of VAUX BUIN.

J.E. GOUGH. Brig. General.
S.G.S.O., 1st Army Corps.

Issued at 8 p.m.

Copies to :-

    1st Division.
    2nd Division.
    3rd Cavalry Brigade.
    5th Cavalry Brigade.
    O.C. Signals.
    A.D.C. for G.O.C.
    S.G.S.O.
    G.S.O. (1).
    D.A. & Q.M.G.
    A.A. & Q.M.G.
    War Diary.
    Office.
    1st Divnl. Amm: Column.
    2nd Divnl. Amm: Column.
    Camp Commandant.

	...ode		This message is on a/c of:	Recd. at
Origin and Service Instructions.		Sent		Date
	At	m.	Service.	From
	To			
	By		(Signature of "Franking Officer.")	By

TO	4th Hussar	3rd Bde. R.H.A
	5th Lancers	
	18th Cavs.	

Sender's Number	Day of Month	In reply to Number	
R.H. 12	31		AAA

1. [illegible] Cavalry [illegible] to have crossed the OISE north of COMPIÈGNE [illegible]...

2. The 1st Cav. Bde. 3rd Cav. Bde. [illegible]...
   [illegible] ... SANCY — VILLERS St. [illegible] ST LA REINE — HAUTE-VILLERS — [illegible] — [illegible]

3. 5. Brigade [illegible] ... at 9.30 am
   1st Squad in the hollow to [illegible] N.W of MORTE-FONTAINE ... loop of L'Isle de Reux and the land near MORTEN Rd. ST. NICOLAS [illegible] to MORTEMONT / HAUTE FONTAINE — MONTIGNY LENCERAIN
   Remainder of Brigade just South of MORTEFONT VILLAGE.

From			
Place			
Time			

The above may be forwarded as now corrected. (Z)

Censor. Signature of Addressor or person authorised to telegraph in his name.

* This line should be erased if not required.

"A" Form. Army Form C. 2121.

MESSAGES AND SIGNALS.

No. of Message

Prefix .... Code .... m. | Words | Charge

Office of Origin and Service Instructions.

Sent

At .... m.

To ....

By ....

This message is on a/c of:

.... *Service.*

(Signature of "Franking Officer.")

Recd. at .... m.

Date ....

From ....

By ....

TO

Sender's Number	Day of Month	In reply to Number	AAA
*			

4 Led Horses – At 4.30 a.m. the led horses
and dismounted men of all units to assemble
at the Road junction at [illegible] ST NICHOLAS
they will be marshalled by Capt. [illegible] –
A.D.C. who will march them to [illegible]
[illegible]
[illegible]
5 [illegible] MOR[illegible]
[illegible] at 4.30 a.m.

6 The Main Body [illegible] Cavalry Brigade [illegible]
[illegible] at 4.30 a.m.

Issued at 8.30 pm   R.H. [illegible] Maj
B.M.

From

Place

Time

The above may be forwarded as now corrected.

Censor.

(Z)

Signature of Addressor or person authorised to telegraph in his name.

* This line should be erased if not required.

Copy No. 7

1st ARMY CORPS OPERATION ORDER No. 5.

31st August, 1914.

Hostile cavalry is reported to have crossed the OISE north of COMPIEGNE moving east, and a strong hostile force is to the north-west of COMPIEGNE.
Our 3rd Cavalry Brigade is round CHELLES, and the 3rd Division is between VILLERS COTTERETS and VAUMMOISE.
Belgian cavalry and artillery are on our eastern flank.

The march will be continued at 4 a.m. tomorrow.
1st Division, starting point VERTE FEUILLE FARM by VILLERS COTTERETS and billet in depth between VILLERS COTTERETS and BOURNVILLE one mile south of LA FERTE MILLON.
2nd Division, starting point southern exit of COUCY by VIVIERES – ROND DE LA REINE – HALTE – VILLERS COTTERETS – PISSELEUX – BOURSONNE – THURY-en-VALOYS.
Local guides should be obtained, and an officer should be sent to Headquarters to obtain further information as to roads and billeting areas at 6 a.m. tomorrow.
5th Cavalry Brigade to cover the rear and east flank.
3rd Cavalry Brigade to cover the west flank.
5th Cavalry Brigade will report to G.O.C. 3rd Cavalry Brigade at HOUTE FONTAINE for further orders.
Both brigades will billet in the area COYOLLES – VAUCIENNES – IVORS. *Thury*
Transport should be sent off as early as possible by the roads allotted to the 1st and 2nd Divisions.
Divisional Ammunition Columns to MAREUIL-sur-OURCQ.

Rendezvous at railhead.

Reports to CHATEAU, one mile west of VILLERS COTTERETS after 5 p.m. *31st August*

J.E. GOUGH, Brig. General.

S.G.S.O., 1st Army Corps.

NOTE:– There will be a long halt from 9 a.m. to 2 p.m.

Issued at 5 p.m.

Copies to :–

1st Division.
2nd Division.
3rd Cavalry Brigade.
5th Cavalry Brigade.
O.C. Signals.
A.D.C. for G.O.C.
S.G.S.O.
G.S.O. (1)
D.A. & Q.M.G.
A. & Q. Office
War Diary.
Camp Commandant.
Office.

Soucy

1st Cavalry Division

Transferred about 15th September 1914 to 2nd Cav Division

B. H. Q.

3rd CAVALRY BRIGADE

SEPTEMBER 1914

Army Form C. 2118

WAR DIARY
or
INTELLIGENCE SUMMARY.
(Erase heading not required.)

WAR DIARY.

3rd Cavalry Brigade

September 1st ———— September 30th 1914.

R M Cawley Major
FM
3rd Cav Bde

WAR DIARY
or
INTELLIGENCE SUMMARY.
(Erase heading not required.)

Army Form C. 2118.

Hour, Date, Place	Summary of Events and Information	Remarks and references to Appendices
ROY ST NICHOLAS Sept 1st 4.30 a.m.	The 3rd Cav Bde assembled about MONTEFONTAINE at 4.30 a.m. 1 Troop 16th Lancers at farm de POUY and 1 Troop at ROY ST NICHOLAS.	1st Corps Operation order No 5 & 3rd Cav Bde order (BM12-3/8/)
	The Brigade acted as Rear guard to the 1st Corps and went into billets at ANTILLY and THURY about 7 pm	PTC
7 pm	Capt McCALLUM joined 9th Hussars from G.H.Q.	
ANTILLY. Sept 2nd 4.30 a.m.	The Brigade was disposed as follows:— 5th Lancers & D Battery huts of BETZ. patrol to BARCY. 9th Hussars, 16th Lancers & E Battery East of ANTILLY. Party ANTILLY patrols to CUVERGNON and Bois de WALIGNY.	1st Corps Operation Order No 5.
5.15 a.m.	9th Hussars & E Battery to ETAVIGNY to cover our retreat — 16th Lancers with 16th Lancers.	
5.30 a.m.	Touch gained with 5th Cav Bde at VILLENEUVE.	
7.0 a.m.	Our Infantry started to fall back from CUVERGNON.	
9.0 a.m.	We started to fall back from CUVERGNON on ST OWEN farm, 5th Lancers on B de MONTROLLES.	
10.0 a.m.	Main body via ETAVIGNY — ACY — NOGEON farm.	
11.0 a.m.	arrived NOGEON farm.	
12.0 (noon)	Enemy shelled tail of 5th Lancers South of MONTROLLES.	
12.15 p.m.	About 6 or 8 Squadrons of hostile Cavalry approached BOUILLANCY from the North, on our shelling them they did not come on.	
1.10 p.m.	Marched to CHAMP FLEURY farm where the Brigade concentrated at 2.30 p.m.	
3.30 p.m.	Started for billets.	
4.30 p.m.	at BARCY met column of 2nd Divn.	
8.0 p.m.	arrived in billets at VILLEMOY.	PTC

Army Form C. 2118.

WAR DIARY
or
INTELLIGENCE SUMMARY.
(Erase heading not required.)

Instructions regarding War Diaries and Intelligence Summaries are contained in F. S. Regs., Part II. and the Staff Manual respectively. Title pages will be prepared in manuscript.

Hour, Date, Place	Summary of Events and Information	Remarks and references to Appendices
VILLEROY. Sep 3rd	Operation order No 7 (1st Corps) & 3rd Cav Bde operation order No 11.	attached.
4.30 a.m.	Brigade left VILLEROY for PENCHARD — Part of 3rd Div still there.	
6.15 a.m.	Sent out advanced guard to seize high ground Point 115 (2 miles N.E of CHAMBRY): Sent out 3 Patrols of 1 officer & 12 men each.	
	(1) 4th Hussars (Lt. Heyman) to RAPERIE to reconnoitre through MARCILLY and CHAMP FLEURY FARM.	
	(2) 5th Lancers (Lt. Rohan) to ETREPILLY to reconnoitre along the road to the halte and TROCY.	
	(3) 16th Lancers (Lt. Clarke) to GUEATRESMES to reconnoitre main road leading from MAY to MULTIEN and road leading from LIZY.	
7.0 a.m.	Dispositions as follows:—	
	[sketch: BARCY ⚬ 4H—4H .115 5L 16L 11 4H → VARREDDES]	
	Found a battalion Scots Guards at .115 acting as Rear guard, who left for VARREDDES at 7.30 a.m.	
7.15 a.m.	ETREPILLY and TROCY clear.	
Between 8–9 a.m.	Small Uhlan patrols were reported all along our front, but they did not push in at all.	
10.0 a.m.	Left the Ridge. (16th R.H.A. & .115).	
10.30 a.m.	Crossed the bridge at GERMIGNY and went for orders.	
12 (noon)	Arrived on main Road in Bois de MAUX.	
3.30 p.m.	Met orders to go into billets at MONTCEISE chateau.	
5.30 p.m.	Arrived at the Chateau, and bivouacked, the Brigade found it.	

Army Form C. 2118.

WAR DIARY
or
INTELLIGENCE SUMMARY.
(Erase heading not required.)

Instructions regarding War Diaries and Intelligence Summaries are contained in F. S. Regs., Part II. and the Staff Manual respectively. Title pages will be prepared in manuscript.

Hour, Date, Place		Summary of Events and Information	Remarks and references to Appendices
MONTIE-BIJE Chateau	Sep 2d.	Received orders for 16th Bde to move via PERREUSE Chateau towards	
	2. am	VOUARRE. – G.O.C. to report to 1st Corps for orders.	
	6.0 am	The Bde left for LE GRAND GRAIRET under Lt-Col BREEKS.	
		A.H.R. ordered us to move to LE FAYET and there await orders, pushing	
		out patrols to the East.	
LE FAYET	9.00 am	LE FAYET – Patrols to DOUE – bot of LA LOGE, LES BERGERES,	
		HAUT MENIL.	
	10.30 am	Got D'l'nal Communication with 5th Cav Bde at DOUE hill.	
	12.30 pm	5th Cav Bde report hostile Columns of all arms moving from BOISSEREZ	
		on VIELMAISONS, and hostile Cavalry moving through BOITRON.	
	1.20 pm	5th Cav Bde report no French at REBAIS – 2000 French left there at	
		2 am for MONTMIRAIL and NOGENT.	
	2.05 pm	5th Cav 3rd Bde report 2 Regiments of Cavalry and a Battery marching	
		towards REBAIS.	
	3.0 pm	Moved 5th Lancers & LE Bailly via HAUT MENIL and MONT BERREUX	
		to watch the REBAIS – BOISSY Road.	
	4.30 pm	Called in 5th Lancers – not required by 5th Cav. Bde.	
	5.0 pm	Enemy brought a Battery on to DOUE hill, on which we opened with	
		our guns. Enemy replied, artillery duel for 3/4 of an hour.	
AULNOY	6.0 pm	Ceased fire and bivac'd on our Infantry outposts at AULNOY and	
		tence to our hills at CHAILLY.	
CHAILLY	6.0 pm	Arrived at CHAILLY – billeted as follows.	
		HQ – 16th Lancers – RHA – CHAILLY.	
		4th Hussars – MONTIGNY	
		5th Lancers – ST PIERRE	

WAR DIARY
or
INTELLIGENCE SUMMARY.
(Erase heading not required.)

Army Form C. 2118.

Hour, Date, Place	Summary of Events and Information	Remarks and references to Appendices
September 5th 1914. CHAILLY.	Bde ordered to act as Rear guard to 1st Corps – 1st Division to be clear of COULOMMIERS	
4.30am	ordered the Brigade to assemble at Pt 164 west of ST PIERRE at 5.15am. Left our Billets.	
5.30am	Sent 9th Hussars and 'E' Battery to FAREMOUTIERS & LA CELLE to cover rear of 2nd Div. Remainder of Brigade disposed as follows. 2 Troops 16th Lancers at LES PARICHETS } Patrols into valley. 2 " " " ST AUGUSTIN } "D" Battery in action – 2 guns E in Reserve. Remainder of 16th & 5th Lancers in Reserve.	
ST AUGUSTIN 8am	1 tp. 5th Lancers for ST AUGUSTIN, having previously sent back 5th Lancers and 2 guns.	
9.30am	Left for LES BORDES, having seen all the Infantry of rearguard well away.	
LES BORDES 10.15am	Arrived at No hindrance to Nt WOOD of LES BORDES.	
2pm	Retired through HAUTEFEUILLE on PEZARCHES and waited for orders. " " back to VILBERT to Billets.	

WAR DIARY
or
INTELLIGENCE SUMMARY.
(Erase heading not required.)

Army Form C. 2118.

Instructions regarding War Diaries and Intelligence Summaries are contained in F.S. Regs., Part II. and the Staff Manual respectively. Title pages will be prepared in manuscript.

Hour, Date, Place	Summary of Events and Information	Remarks and references to Appendices
September 6th 1914. VILBERT	Army operation order – and Troops. Copy of 3rd Cav. Bde order 5th Cav Bde. placed under orders of Genl. Gough.	attached.
5:30 am	G.H.Q. reported a German Corps about MOUROUX ordered 3rd Cav Bde to attendre at CHAMPLET-5th - - - Sud of Chateau de la FORTELLE.	
6:30 am	12 Lancers at PEZARCHES had their advanced troop at TOUQUIN driven in by shell fire. Later the whole Regiment was driven in in RIGNY, but enemy's advance was checked by artillery fire. Assembled both Brigades 1 mile East of MARLES.	
1pm		
3pm	Heard that the Germans were leaving houlx.	
3:15pm	Sent 1 Sqd 16th Lancers on through LUMIGNY to PEZARCHES, 1 Sqd on FAREMOUTIERS. Moved the Brigade up to LUMIGNY and then on to PEZARCHES, with 16th Lancers as advanced guard.	
5:30pm	Found a Machine Gun at the top of the Foret de MALVOISINE and sent up a section R.H.A. to clear them out. 16th Lancers gradually worked their way up to their line PARADIS – LE TARTRE – had some horses shot.	
6:30pm	Started to billet as follows: – 16th Lancers – PARADIS – 5th Lancers & R.H.A. PEZARCHES – 9th Hussars TOUQUIN.	
7pm	Advanced Guard 5th Cav. Bde. arrived, sent in 1 Regt. to relieve the outposts of the 16th Lancers. Later 16th reported FAREMOUTIERS and MAUPERTHUIS clear, enemy retreating north.	
LUMIGNY PEZARCHES		

WAR DIARY
or
INTELLIGENCE SUMMARY.
(Erase heading not required.)

Army Form C. 2118.

Hour, Date, Place	Summary of Events and Information	Remarks and references to Appendices
September 7th 1914. PEZARCHES	No operation orders.	
4.30 am	Sent 16th Lancers & 11cc RHA to occupy high ground south of Coulommiers with patrols through that place and Boissy and Chailly. 4th Hussars to send officers patrol to Amillis – all Infantry actually halt.	
PARADIS. 7.30am	Brigade H/Qrs for PARADIS.	
EPIEDS 8.25am	" " " EPIEDS	
9.30am	Ordered 5th Cav. Bde to PARADIS. Received orders that there was to be a great advance to the line DAGNY – COULOMMIERS – MAISON CELLES. When the Infantry would be at 10 am. and that the 3rd & 5th Cav Bdes where to cover the front of the army and get in touch with the French Cavalry on the C/V. (?). Ordered the 3rd Cav Bde to Point 154 – LES PUYTS – MONTIGNY on BOISSY. 5th Cav Bde via LA MÉE farm on CHAILLY and LES LIMONS.	
12 (noon)	When passing LES PUYTS German guns opened on us from our pocket BOISSY. We brought our guns into action and silenced the hostile Battery. Then we saw at least 1 Cav Regt with Infantry beyond retiring low out of BOISSY towards REBAIS – Shelled them well.	
1 pm.	Advanced 4th Hussars through MONTIGNY, remainder of Brigade through CHAILLY. Turned off the 5th Cav Bde on CHAUFFRY and ST DENIS. Very intricate Country – deep valley – thick orchards and villages.	
4 pm.	Arrived LES GRANGES – Troops to MAZAGRAN. Small hotel patrols in each place. Sent 4th Hussars on to reconnoitre REBAIS – SAULSOY – DOUE.	
4.10 pm.	Received G.H.Q. order timed 11.10 am that the whole army was advancing to the line BEAUVAIS – REBAIS – DOUE. No infantry been yet.	

Army Form C. 2118.

WAR DIARY
or
INTELLIGENCE SUMMARY.
(Erase heading not required.)

Instructions regarding War Diaries and Intelligence Summaries are contained in F. S. Regs., Part II. and the Staff Manual respectively. Title pages will be prepared in manuscript.

Hour, Date, Place	Summary of Events and Information	Remarks and references to Appendices
6 pm.	9th Hussars reported hostile patrols in MAZAGRAN and LES MARCHES but they retired.	
6.30 pm.	Heard from 5th Cav Bde that they were in REBAIS during not with Cavalry.	
7.0 pm.	Started to biller in the area VILLENEUVE - VINOT - MAZAGRAN with advanced regiment in CHANTREINE and LES MARCHES.	
8 pm.	Heard that the 5th Cav Bde about ST DENIS, with advanced Regiment in REBAIS. AF JHussars in LES MARCHES were in contact with the Enemy - but the latter retired later.	Rpto.
9 pm.	Brigade Headquarters MAZAGRAN.	

WAR DIARY
or
INTELLIGENCE SUMMARY.
(Erase heading not required.)

Army Form C. 2118.

Hour, Date, Place	Summary of Events and Information	Remarks and references to Appendices
September 8th 1914. MAZAGRAN.	Army Operation order No. 18 and Brigade order No. 2 (attached). The 3rd & 5th Cav Bde to cover the front. Ordered 3rd Bde on MOUROY to cross the Retht MORIN at ST CYR - 5th Cav Bde on GIBRALTAR to cross at ORLY or ST OUEN; to total at 5.30 am.	
5.30 am.	Head near DOUE was clear.	
MOUROY. 7am.	Arrived at MOUROY - Sent 5th Lancers into ST CYR, and haughtrup D battery into action against retreating enemy on north Bank; very difficult to see owing to woods, but the dust of heavy Column could be seen. Later. Enemy opened on us from about ROHENY and S.W of BOULIERES. Haughtrup 'E' Battery - Enemy; shell fire heavy and very accurate; 5th Lancers were fired to retire from ST CYR being a cross fire.	
9am.	The Infantry of the advanced guard of the 5th Div. arrived (13th Bde). head of the road but did not push on into the wood.	
9.30am.	Sent back for some more batteries.	
10 am.	I went over to see Sir Charles FERGUSSON & ask him to push up his Infantry to clear the valley. He said he had ordered his 13th Bde on ST CYR and his 14th Bde on ST OUEN, he was waiting for the latter to commence his attack. He was hesitant about his left flank as he could not hear of the 3rd Corps, and asked us to move as to his left flank to fill the gap. We had presently the front to patrol to get in touch with the 3rd Corps. I told him we would do so as soon as we could extricate our guns. Long Tom fired from DOUE hill.	

WAR DIARY
or
INTELLIGENCE SUMMARY.

(Erase heading not required.)

Army Form C. 2118.

Hour, Date, Place	Summary of Events and Information	Remarks and references to Appendices
MOUROY (Cont'd)	We sent the 5th Lancers at once to LA CHEVIE FARM and got in 'E' Battery. 'D' Battery had been badly mauled. Major GILLSON being wounded and Lieut. GOUGH and PARKER killed.	
1pm	We got in D' Battery as the Infantry had started to attack ST CYR and SIOUEN.	
LE GRAND CLAIRET 2.30 pm	We moved off towards LE GRAND CLAIRET when the Brigade arrived about 2.30 pm, and reported to General SNOW (4th Dvsn.) who was there. He asked us to stay where we were but to send 2 troops to General WILSON to help him patrol. He had ordered his Infantry to attack the village of ST MARTIN and COURCELLES. The B.M. went into Billets taken as follows.	
	5th Lancers ROMENY	
	16th " PERREUVE Chateau.	
	4th Hussars } LE GRAND CLAIRET.	
	Bde H.Q. } LE PETIT	
	RHA and Amm. Col. L'HOTEL des BOIS.	
9pm	Buried Lieuts GOUGH and PARKER, RHA, at L'HOTEL des BOIS.	PMC

WAR DIARY or INTELLIGENCE SUMMARY

Army Form C. 2118.

Hour, Date, Place	Summary of Events and Information	Remarks and references to Appendices
September 9th 1914. LE GRAND GLAIRET.	Army Operation Order No.19. & Cav. Bde Order (attached) ordered to Cover 2nd Corps and get in touch with the French Army. Major Campbell's Sqdn 16th Lancers sent to 5th Divn as Divisional Cavalry until relieved by 19th Innisrt.	
PERREUSE Chateau	The Brigade was ordered to wait until the Infantry had crossed the LA FERTE Bridge.	
3 pm.	We saw a large trek of Germans moving N.E from JAIGNES, too far off for our guns. No sign of being able to Cross at LA FERTE so asked the 2nd Corps for news of the 5th Divn. — Having that they had got across at MERY and MANTEUIL, we saddled up and marched via JOUARRE and COURCELLES to ROUGEVILLE when we arrived about 6 pm.	
4 pm.		
ROUGEVILLE 6 pm.	We got expected to get 2nd Corps for orders. The Brigade went into billets as follows. HQ & 5th Lancers - GRAND Mt MENARD 16th Lancers - CHANT MANENE 4th Innisd - VILLARE RHA } Amm Col. } - ROUGEVILLE. Fd Amb } Captain B. FAIRFAX, Reserve of officers, joined for duty, and placed in charge of "A" Echelon, 1st Line Transport.	RJMc

WAR DIARY
or
INTELLIGENCE SUMMARY.

(Erase heading not required.)

Army Form C. 2118.

Hour, Date, Place	Summary of Events and Information	Remarks and references to Appendices
Sepr. 10th 1914. ROUGEVILLE	Army Operation order No 20 (attached).	
9.45 am	The Brigade Marched via SAACY-NANTEUIL-BEZU-VENTELET FARM to PLATRIERE, where we arrived about 7 am after having been blocked by the 3rd Bde.	
6.30 am	Ordered 5th Cav Bde to PREMONT on CHEZY. 8th Cav Bde on GERMIGNY and GANDELU.	
Later	Heard from 5th Cav Bde of large tks of Germans on the CHEZY Ridge. Too far to bring our batteries into action and so pushed forward to the GANDELU Ridge. The 12th Lancers and Scots Greys galloped the Ridge under cover of the artillery and captured 200 prisoners - killed about 70 more, took 5 machine guns, 1 Field gun and several wagons. Several German stragglers left in the woods about BRUMETZ and GANDELU who bushed our men. Lieut Shrard 4th Hussars being killed.	
1 pm	Advanced through BRUMETZ and sent out reconnaissances.	
6 pm	Assembled the 2 Brigades near DAMMARD. The Brigades went into billets as follows 3rd Cav Bde MARIZY and MOLSOY 5th Cav Bde PASSY and MACOGNY.	

WAR DIARY
or
INTELLIGENCE SUMMARY.
(Erase heading not required.)

Army Form C. 2118.

Hour, Date, Place	Summary of Events and Information	Remarks and references to Appendices
September 11th 1914. MARIZY.	Army Operation Order No. 21 and Cav.B.d. Order No. 3 (attached)	
9.0 am	Sent out the following	
	½ Sqdn 5th Lancers to NOROY	
	½ " 16th " to CHOUY.	
5.0 am	3 officers Patrols	
	① VILLERS - HELON - VIERZY.	
	② BILLY - ST REMY - BUZANCY.	
	③ LE PLESSIER HULEU - HARTENNES - DROIZY.	
6.0 am	3rd Cav Bde on NOROY	
	5th Cav Bde on CHOUY.	
7.0 am	3rd Cav Bde Point 180	
8.45 am	" " BLANZY	
	5th Cav Bde LE PLESSIER HULEU.	
	Later moved on to Point 157 VILLEMONTOIRE with 1 Regt at BUZANCY	
	Patrols reported Infantry entrenching North of NOYANT and SEPTMONTS	
	Confirmed by personal reconnaissance.	very heavy rain
2.30 pm	Heard an outburst of fire towards CHAUDUN, found Kohit-kai the French	
	attacking some Germans who had come out of SOISSONS.	
	Moved the Brigade nearer in order to cooperate. The rain was	
	heavy we could see very little. When it cleared we opened with	
	a battery on where the French shells were falling. The shooting died	
	away and the Brigade went into Billets as follows.	
7 pm	H.Q. TIGNY - RHA TIGNY - 4th Hussars & 16th Lancers VILLEMONTOIRE	
	5th Lancers CHARANTIGNY.	

Army Form C. 2118.

WAR DIARY
or
INTELLIGENCE SUMMARY.
(Erase heading not required.)

Instructions regarding War Diaries and Intelligence Summaries are contained in F. S. Regs., Part II. and the Staff Manual respectively. Title pages will be prepared in manuscript.

Hour, Date, Place	Summary of Events and Information	Remarks and references to Appendices
September 12th 1914. T16 N.Y.	Circular Order No 22 (army) and Cav. 13th order No 7 (attached).	Very wet day.
9 am	The Brigade started a march at 9.30 am through BUZANCY.	
5 am	9th Hussars and 1st RHA as left flank guard BUZANCY – d'JEGUIRY. Sent 12 5th Lancers via CHACRISE to AMBRIEF and then to BOIS de SOISSON's Farm, while the remainder of the Brigade marched through NAMPTEUIL on BOIS de SOISSONS FARM. The 5th Lancers were then sent on to CIRY and from thee to CHAVENEY. The Bridges at CONDÉ and PAILLY over the AISNE being held. Sent on 9th Hussars and Section RHA to attack the bridge at VAILLY and took Command of the Brigade to the high ground N.E. of CHAVENEY.	
3.30 pm	Brought 9 guns into action against a Battery & natural shelling. The 9th Hussars when a hostile Infantry advance was made against us from BRENELLE. The machine guns of the 5th and 16th Lancers came into action and the 2 dismounted troops of the 16th Lancers to hold the edge of a wood in the Cyr flank. The remainder of the 16th and the 5th Lancers moved round mounted to our left. Brought a battery into action against the front of the Infantry and moved another Section to our left to enfilade them. Sent to 5th Cav 13th to ask them to co-operate	
4.30 pm	via BRENELLE. The German Infantry put up the white flag. 101 Prisoners surrendered. They were Landwehr troops. They left several killed and wounded, including 3 officers, the major being killed.	
6 pm	The Brigade billeted at CHAVENEY and CIRY.	

WAR DIARY
or
INTELLIGENCE SUMMARY.
(Erase heading not required.)

Army Form C. 2118.

Hour, Date, Place	Summary of Events and Information	Remarks and references to Appendices
CHESSAMY. Sepr 13th 1914. 4.30 am.	Received Army Operation Order No 28. And 2nd Army Corps order No 23. } attached.	
5.40 am.	Issued Cav. Bde Order No 7.	
5.0 am.	G.O.C wrote G.1. to G.H.Q, answered by A.O 908. (attached). and G.2. to II. Corps, answered by 9.55 (attached). Received the Composition of the 2nd Cav. Divn.	
10.0 am.	As the Bridges over the AISNE were either destroyed or held by the Enemy and there was no question of the Brigades being able to cross, the 3rd Cav. Bde remained in Billets. The Enemy opened with heavy howitzers on our heavy battery above CIRY. The 16th Lancers therefore saddled up and moved up the hill to EPRITEL Farm. At CHESSAMY was also shelled, the 11th and Amm Column moved out under cover of the hill. The 5th Lancers and 19th Hussars and Bde HQ remained in their billets. During the day the 2nd Corps attacked the villages and ridges at MAILLY and CONDÉ. During the afternoon we were ordered to be ready to go across in the evening to fill the gap between the 3rd Divn. and 1st Corps - but as the troops were not passable by Cavalry - this was not of the question.	

Army Form C. 2118.

WAR DIARY
or
INTELLIGENCE SUMMARY.
(Erase heading not required.)

Instructions regarding War Diaries and Intelligence Summaries are contained in F.S. Regs., Part II. and the Staff Manual respectively. Title pages will be prepared in manuscript.

Hour, Date, Place		Summary of Events and Information	Remarks and references to Appendices
CHASSEMY.	Sept 13th 1914.	Remained in our billets for the remainder of the day.	Very wet.
CHATEAU CHASSEMY. Sept 14th 1914.		During the night received Army Operation order No 22. and 2nd Corps Operation order No 24. } attached. Issued Operation order (2nd Cav Div.) No 8 And after order B.M. 5, after hearing from the 3rd Div. at what time the Bridge at VAILLY would be ready for us to cross over. Ordered the 5th Cav: Bde to cross the bridge at 6 am and the 3rd Cav Bde to follow it.	
VAILLY BRIDGE.	6.30 am	Owing to a delay in getting their orders the 5th Cav Bde did not arrive till 6.30 am. They immediately pushed across the pontoon bridge, but before the 3rd Cav Regt. (20th Hussars) had got across the Thick mist zone and the Germans started shelling the Bridge with a 6" Howitzer and a Battery of field guns. The remainder of the Brigade was stopped from crossing, and the 3rd Cav: Bde got into the Park at CHASSEMY Chateau, off the main road. As they turn no tum to shelter the 3 Regiments in VAILLY village the 20th Hussars were brought back over the Bridge. The infantry were found to be holding only the ridge of the hills within a quarter of a mile of the river.	
	11 am	Later as the village of VAILLY was being heavily shelled it was decided about 11 am to bring back the 12th Lancers and Greys by troops across the bridge.	

Army Form C. 2118.

WAR DIARY
or
INTELLIGENCE SUMMARY.
(Erase heading not required.)

Instructions regarding War Diaries and Intelligence Summaries are contained in F.S. Regs., Part II. and the Staff Manual respectively. Title pages will be prepared in manuscript.

Hour, Date, Place	Summary of Events and Information	Remarks and references to Appendices
VAILLY (Cont'd)	They had a very hot time as they crossed the ridge and the open stretch of road up to the wood. Four shells bursting into each troop as it passed. 3 officers of the Scots Greys were hit and a few men, as well as about 20 horses.	
12.30pm	As there was becoming such a block of troops in the Chateau park, it was decided to move the brigades up through the woods to the top of the hill near BRENELLE. The enemy was searching the woods as we went up, and the Temper-HICKS, 16th Lancers wounded. On arrival at the top of the hill we found several batteries in action being shelled by the 6th howitzers. The brigade was collected - patrols sent out - and a gun position reconnoitred. In the meantime the 3rd and 13th Ammunition Column, 2nd Cav Fd Ambulance and "B" Echelon was parked in and about CHASSEMY village. The enemy started shelling the village and the Ammn Col. had to leave the wagons and take horses and lines to cover. They lost 12 horses. The 16th and a "B" Echelon also had several mules very badly shot.	
2.30pm	2 troops 16th Lancers and a Machine Gun were sent towards the Butts at CHIVONNE	
5.30pm	The Brigade left the hills for billets. HQ at LIME, with the 16th Lancers - Ambn: Col. 3rd & 13th RHA and Transport. 5th Lancers at QUINCEY - A Sqdn at MONTIGNSARAM	MJJC

(9.26.6) W 257—076 100,000 4/12 H W V 79/3208

Army Form C. 2118.

WAR DIARY
or
INTELLIGENCE SUMMARY.

(Erase heading not required.)

Instructions regarding War Diaries and Intelligence Summaries are contained in F.S. Regs., Part II. and the Staff Manual respectively. Title pages will be prepared in manuscript.

Hour, Date, Place	Summary of Events and Information	Remarks and references to Appendices
LIME. Sept 15th 1914.	During the night received Army Operation Order No 26. Issued orders. (BM1.-15/9/14) and BM 2.	{ attached
6.30 am	The Brigade assembled in a position of readiness as mentioned in orders, with troops 19th XVth Hussars and the Bde Machine Guns in the Chassemy Woods. The Brigade remained in its position all day, with the exception of its batteries which came into action to ascertain ranges, though observation was very difficult.	
5pm	The Brigade returned to billets —
H.Q. — 3rd Bde R.H.A. & Ammn Col. } LIME
16th Lancers & A & B Echelon }
19th Hussars — BRAINE
5th Lancers — QUINCEY.	RNK

79 / 3298

WAR DIARY
or
INTELLIGENCE SUMMARY.
(Erase heading not required.)

Army Form C. 2118.

Hour, Date, Place	Summary of Events and Information	Remarks and references to Appendices
LIME. 16/9/14.	During the night received Army Operation orders No 26. and 2nd Corps Operation order No 25. Issued 2nd Cav. Bde. operation order No 9 and B.M 2	Filed
6 am	The Brigade were ordered to assemble in the same place as yesterday (Farm) Sent to all Units to stand fast in their billets till 8a.m, owing to the rain. A Staff officer of the 3rd Bde. came to see us to ask us to watch the bridge at CONDÉ by day and to bar the roads leading from it by night. Sent for Genl CHETWODE and a Sqdn Leader and two 2nd field troops. Also a Squadron Leader from the 16th Lancers. Asked the 5th Cav Bde to send a Sqdn to reconnoitre the bridge over the VESLE on the CIRY-CONDÉ road, and to make arrangements for holding it in a state of defence before nightfall, and to occupy it at night. (Cap.n HODGES Squadron 20th Hussars - with the Regimental Machine guns). Cap.n NERVES Sq.n 16th Lancers with Machine guns was to do the same thing in the CHASSEMY-CONDÉ road at Village of Petitend.	Very wet morning
8.95 am	As it had cleared up the 2 Brigades were ordered to treat their places of assembly at 10 a.m.	
10 am	Gen.l VAUGHAN arrived to take over the 3rd Cav Bde. as the General was shifting the place of assembly of the 3rd Cav Bde the 7 Brigade were assembled behind the wood half a mile further south. D. Battery was placed in action behind a wood ½ mile to the north.	
10·30am	General Gough & Vaughan took out to make a personal reconnaissance. The situation much the same as yesterday, but much less shelling.	

WAR DIARY
or
INTELLIGENCE SUMMARY.

(Erase heading not required.)

Army Form C. 2118.

Instructions regarding War Diaries and Intelligence Summaries are contained in F.S. Regs., Part II. and the Staff Manual respectively. Title pages will be prepared in manuscript.

Hour, Date, Place	Summary of Events and Information	Remarks and references to Appendices
	During the morning the 4th Hussars collected about 100 Infantry stragglers in BAVAI and 20 men and horses belonging to 1st 11th Cav. Bde.	
3 pm	About 3 pm 2 men of the 20th Hussars galloped in to say that their troop had been fired on by a machine gun on the PETIT Bridge and dispersed. Lieutenant Major Campbell 16th Lancers to clear up the situation, who found the 20th Hussar Squadron perfectly quiet and happy and so they returned.	
3.45 pm	A German aeroplane flew over the Brigade, and so the Regiment was sent back to reconnoitre.	
5.30 pm	As everything seemed quiet the Brigade was ordered to return to villers.	
6.30 pm	Issued orders for next day. The 5th Lancers to relieve the 16th Lancer Squadron at 6.30 am on the CHARLEROI - CONDE road, the remainder of the Brigade to remain in their billets.	
8.45 pm	Heard that the 20th Hussar Squadron was being attacked at 7.30 pm, and at the same time heard from Capt. O'NEAVE that all was quiet.	

WAR DIARY
or
INTELLIGENCE SUMMARY.
(Erase heading not required.)

Army Form C. 2118.

Hour, Date, Place	Summary of Events and Information	Remarks and references to Appendices
LIME. 17/9/14.		
6.30 am	Captain NEWE's Squadron 16th Lancers relieved by Capt HENLEY'S Squadron 5th Lancers, on the CHASSEMY – CONDÉ Road. The remainder of the Brigade remaining in Billets.	Fine wet day.
8.0 am	The G.O.C. and Bethmayer went in to BRAINE to see the G.O.C. 3rd Division, to get the situation from him. arranged with him that he should shell the Bridge at CONDÉ at 12 (noon) to enable him & to get our patrols nearer to reconnoitre the Bridge. Then we rode round to the outpost squadron, which was in trenches at the western Edge of the CHASSEMY wood.	
12 – 1 pm	Lieut COULTER, 5th Lancers reported that he had got within 100x of the Bridge which he reported intact, and that there was another bridge an iron one 250x further up the river. (This must be the bridge over the canal, not over the AISNE). Bril-Bethputn to got 3rd Divn. The Situation remained as yesterday	
6.95 pm	Issued Brigade operation order No 12. (attached)	
7.30 pm	Received a report from Capt. HENLEY outpost Sqdn. Enemy Cased shelling CHASSEMY from 10.30 – 6 pm. Some shipping near the guys boat on the VESLE at 8.30 pm. It is close under wall of Middle war on his right. LIEUT DE BURGH who was rations on foot to reconnoitre CONDÉ bridge at 11.15 am had not returned at 6.80 pm. Lt BROCKLEHURST, 10th Indian, joined as ADC to General VAUGHAN. Received Cav Divl Operation order No 2. (attached)	

Army Form C. 2118.

WAR DIARY
or
INTELLIGENCE SUMMARY.
(Erase heading not required.)

Instructions regarding War Diaries and Intelligence Summaries are contained in F.S. Regs., Part II. and the Staff Manual respectively. Title pages will be prepared in manuscript.

Hour, Date, Place		Summary of Events and Information	Remarks and references to Appendices
LIME.	18/9/14. 6 am.	Report from Capt. HENLEY's outpost Sqdn, 5th Lancers. Only a few isolated shots last night from about COTTES. Fire 5.10 a.m. Enemy have been dropping shots in the wood 260° from our M.G. Emplacement. Holding Head of Lieut DE BURGH.	
	6.30 am	The 4.5 Hussars relieved the outpost squadron, and with the remainder of the Regiment acted as support.	
	7.30 am	3rd Hussars sent for Lt COOPER who reconnoitred CONDE Bridge to accompany this G.O.C. to 2nd Corps H.Q. The 4.5 Hussars found that the 5th Cav Bde were not holding the VESLE bridge as ordered. General VAUGHAN went to their H.Q. about it.	
	1.17 pm	4th Hussars report that all was quiet and that a troop 12th Lancers had arrived at the VESLE bridge.	
	4 pm.	a F.G.C.M. held on No.4819. 2nd Cpl CRICK, 18th Lancers for being asleep whilst acting on outpost. Sentenced to 3 years Penal Servitude. Confirmed and sent to G.H.Q. for approval.	
	5.30 pm.	2nd Cav Div informed us that the Div. would probably move in the morning to join the General Reserve (6th Div.).	
	6.30 pm	4.5 Hussars reported all quiet.	
	10 pm.	Received a message today that the 2nd Cav Div had been allotted to the General Reserve, but would remain at present located for the present.	
	10.20pm	Issued BH.33. (attached).	

RHC

WAR DIARY
or
INTELLIGENCE SUMMARY.
(Erase heading not required.)

Army Form C. 2118.

Hour, Date, Place	Summary of Events and Information	Remarks and references to Appendices
LIME. 19/9/14.	The 3rd Cav: Bde remained in its Billets all day.	Wet morning.
1pm.	Hearing that the Machine Gun Detachment 16th Hussars was at LE HAVRE, we applied for them to be attached to the Brigade. Received a reply that they had already been allotted to the 2nd Corps.	
3pm.	G.H.Q. informed us that 1 officer and 48 others would arrive at BRAINE tomorrow for the 4th Hussars.	
	The following officers of the Indian Army joined the 5th Lancers. Captains NUTTING and YATES BROWN, Lieuts ATKINSON and HAWKINS.	
7.15pm	G.H.Q asked how many badges the brigade had destroyed Prize operational Answered Nil.	
7.20pm	2nd Cav Divn ordered us to hand over to Amm Col. 2 SAA carts per Regt. Arranged for this to be done in the morning.	
10.10pm	Received W.Q.12 (19th) – (attached.) Situation unchanged. 6th Divs operation orders BAZOCHES operation orders will not be issued.	
6.45pm	Issued RM 38. (attached)	
	Between 5pm and 8pm. Heavy gun firing and also Machine Gun and rifle fire was heard to the North. It seemed to be coming from the direction of CHAVONNE.	
	Lieut KING (late 16th Lancers) arrived for duty with the 5th Lancers. He was ordered to join the 16th Lancers for duty.	

WAR DIARY or INTELLIGENCE SUMMARY

Army Form C. 2118.

Place	Hour, Date	Summary of Events and Information	Remarks and references to Appendices
LIME	20/9/14	Situation remained the same.	
	7 am.	Received orders from Cav. Bde. to hand 2 S.A.A. Carts per Regiment over to the Ammn. Col. in order to decrease the size of 1st Echelon and to make it more mobile.	
	10.0 am	Received orders from 2nd Cav. Bde. to detail 1 M.G. Section for Temporary Special duty with the 3rd Cav. Bde. at once. Sent the 19th Hussar Section under Lt. SOMERS.	
		During the afternoon we heard that the 2nd Cav. Bde. had been placed at the disposal of the II Corps, whose 3rd Division had been seriously attacked during the night.	
		Received a report on the Hdqrs. over RAISNE. (filed with circulars).	
	6.45 pm	Issued instructions that unless further orders were received the 3rd Cav. Bde. would remain in its billets tomorrow.	RHC
LIME	21/9/14	Situation remained the same.	
		The Brigade remained in its Billets all day - Exercise & grazing. No sign of Reinforcements for 4th Hussars promised yesterday. Captain T. THOMPSON, 4th Hussars, joined his Regiment, without horses.	
		Wrote to Cav. Bde. to report that during the last 2 days - 3 officers had been sent up without horses - asked permission to return them to the Base, and also to him to G.H.Q. to discontinue the practice.	
	6.45 pm	Issued Instructions that unless further orders were received the 3rd Cav. Bde. would remain in its billets tomorrow.	RHC

Army Form C. 2118.

WAR DIARY
or
INTELLIGENCE SUMMARY.
(Erase heading not required.)

Instructions regarding War Diaries and Intelligence Summaries are contained in F.S. Regs., Part II. and the Staff Manual respectively. Title pages will be prepared in manuscript.

Hour, Date, Place		Summary of Events and Information	Remarks and references to Appendices.
LIME	22/9/14	Situation remained the same.	
		Captain S.F.N. THOMPSON, 9th Hussars, Lieut HAWKINS- Indian Army (attached 5th Lancers) Lieut KING. attached 16th Lancers } who had arrived without authority returned to the Advanced Base to get horses to themselves, by order of 2nd Cav: Bde.	
		Captain P.F.GELY. Indian Army, arrived from Reserve Regiment at ROUEN and posted to 5th Lancers for duty.	
	6.45pm	Issued orders that unless further orders were received the 3rd Cav Bde would remain in billets tomorrow.	
	10.0 pm	Received W.G. 10 Sep: 22 from Cav Div. (attached)	PJK.
LIME	23/9/14.	General Situation remained the same.	
	10 am	Received Instructions to be prepared to move about midday — but this was subsequently cancelled.	
	6.45pm	Issued orders that unless further orders were received the 3rd Cav B'de would remain in billets tomorrow.	
	10.0 pm.	Received similar instructions from the Cav Div.	PJK

WAR DIARY
or
INTELLIGENCE SUMMARY.
(Erase heading not required.)

Army Form C. 2118.

Hour, Date, Place	Summary of Events and Information	Remarks and references to Appendices
LIME 24/9/14.	General situation remained the same. The following reinforcements were received. 4th Hussars Lieut LEVITA 2/Lt HUNTER. 90 fully equipped men 90 " horses. 22 Riding " 17 Draft " 6th Lancers 2/Lt J.D. FOWLER 2/Lt E. SCOTT-BROWNE. 90 fully equipped men 90 " horses. 21 Riding " 17 Draft " The new horses arrived in very poor condition. 15 sent to the Veterinary Hospital at BRAINE. The 5th Lancers still require to complete 5 officers, 154 Riding + Pack horses. 133 other Ranks, 9 Draught The DD "B"y RHA took over 5 horses from the Light Draught of the 4th Hussars. 6.30pm Issued instructions that unless further orders were received the 3rd Cav Bde would remain in their bivouacs.	PTO

Army Form C. 2118.

WAR DIARY
or
INTELLIGENCE SUMMARY.

(Erase heading not required.)

Hour, Date, Place	Summary of Events and Information	Remarks and references to Appendices
LIME 25/9/14.	The general situation remained the same. No operation orders issued by 2nd Cav Div.	RHC
LIME 26/9/14. 5 am	Hearing very heavy firing coming from the direction of our 1st Corps - we sent word for the 3rd Cav Bde to assemble at the Cross Roads at LIME at 6.30 am.	
6.30 am	The G.O.C. then motored in to 2nd Cav Div for information.	
9.45 am	Heard that the 1st Corps had repulsed the attacks made on it without calling on its reserves. The 3rd Cav Bde then returned to Billets.	
	2nd Cav Div asked for names of N.C.Os recommended for commission. Worked on Condition - which still seem very vague.	
6.45 pm	Issued instructions that unless further orders were received the Bde would remain in Billets tomorrow - and that Divine Services would be held in BRAINE - LIME and QUINCY.	
	During the morning "D" Battery RHA received the following reinforcements. 14. N.C.O's & men - 2 Officers Chargers - 28 Horses. The horses arrived without saddles or harness. They were very small - too small for draught - but in fair condition.	RHC

WAR DIARY
or
INTELLIGENCE SUMMARY.

(Erase heading not required.)

Army Form C. 2118.

Hour, Date, Place	Summary of Events and Information	Remarks and references to Appendices
LINE. 27/9/14. 5:15 am	Received orders to turn out at once and await further orders. Issued instructions accordingly.	
6:15 am	Heard that at 2.30 am, the enemy were reported to be crossing CONDÉ Bridge in force. That the 5 Cav Bde were to go to SEPMERIES, and that the 3rd Cav Bde were to await further orders.	
7.0 am.	Received orders that the 5th Div. saw no sign of enemy south of the CONDÉ Bridge, and that the above information apparently false, and that the Cavalry were to return to billets.	
12.30 pm	Issued orders that if the Brigade remained in Billets tomorrow, the G.O.C. would inspect the "B" Echelon Transport — With Capt. NUTTING 5th Cavalry takes over today from Capt. BRIDGE. Indian S+T — The latter officer to report to Staff JACK. A.S.C at ORLEANS. 2Lt DRURY, late Intelligence Corps, joined 4th Hussars for duty with small motor car.	
7 pm	Reinforcement for 16th Lancers arrived. Capt. RIDDELL, Lieut. McNEILL, LONGRIDGE and EVANS. 186 men and 285 horses. Too dark tonight to report on their condition. Issued instructions that unless further orders were received the Brigade would remain in Billets. Lt Col. T. BRIDGES joined to take over command of 4th Hussars. Divine Service was held by Capt. Revd GUINESS at the Headquarters of each Cavalry Regt.	

Army Form C. 2118.

WAR DIARY
or
INTELLIGENCE SUMMARY.

(Erase heading not required.)

Instructions regarding War Diaries and Intelligence Summaries are contained in F.S. Regs., Part II. and the Staff Manual respectively. Title pages will be prepared in manuscript.

Hour, Date, Place	Summary of Events and Information	Remarks and references to Appendices
LIME 28/9/14.	General situation remained the same.	
9.30 am.	The G.O.C. inspected the "B" Echelon Transport of the Brigade.	
	The G.O.C. asked for permission to send down to the Base a party consisting of an officer (Capt. Scott, A.S.Hussars) N.C.O's and men, to take over and get fit any remounts allotted to the Brigade.	
7.30 pm.	Received orders that unless further orders were received, Units would remain in their billets tomorrow.	PJM
LIME 29/9/14.	General situation remained the same.	
	During the morning went thoroughly into numbers wanting to complete in the Brigade.	
	We still require about 270 men and 360 horses. (see attached return) Made arrangements to send Capt. Scott, A.S.Hussars, 13 K.H. & 16th Lancers and 16 N.C.O's & men, to the Base to assist at the Remount Depot to take over the next batch of Remounts for the Brigade and get them fit. All the Remounts we had received so far were very unfit, and obviously had received insufficient food and exercise. Many of them bad horses.	
11 pm.	Received orders that the Cavalry Division might have to move to new billets today. Ordered Units to be ready to move at 3/10 m.	
3.15 am	Heard that the move was postponed till tomorrow till tomorrow.	

WAR DIARY
or
INTELLIGENCE SUMMARY.

(Erase heading not required.)

Army Form C. 2118.

Hour, Date, Place		Summary of Events and Information	Remarks and references to Appendices
29/9/14 (cont^d)	7 p.m.	Received H.Q. 4^B 29/9/14 (attached) giving orders for the move to new billets tomorrow.	
	7.30 p.m.	Issued Operation order N°1 (attached). The billets of the Brigade as follows.	
		Bde H.Q. CHACRISE	
		16th Lancers AMBRIEF	
		9th Hussars VIOLAINE	
		5th Lancers MAAST ET VIOLAINE	
		"D" By R.H.A. NAMPTEUIL	
		2nd Cav. Fd Amb. CHACRISE.	
		(Sec "B" Peleton)	
		2nd Cav. Div^l. Headquarters the CHATEAU at HARTENNES.	P.T.O.
LINE 30/9/14.	9 a.m. to 1 a.m.	Billeting parties of units sent on to new billets. Units left their billets independently for their new billets which they reached between 12 and 1 p.m. It was found that VIOLAINE and MAAST ET VIOLAINE were too small for a Regiment - so the 2 villages were handed over to the 16th Lancers and the 9th Hussars sent to CUIRY HOUSE. It was also found that the billeting horse of the 16th and 5th Hussars were waiting in the villages occupied by our Regiments - but arrangements were made to water at different times.	

WAR DIARY or INTELLIGENCE SUMMARY

Hour, Date, Place	Summary of Events and Information	Remarks and references to Appendices
CHACRISE. 30/9/14. (Cont'd).	Received list of French honours awarded to the officers, NCOs and men of the 3rd Cav Bde (attached). 2nd Cav Div: asked for list of officers, NCOs & men to be mentioned in despatches. List of officers forwarded to 2nd Cav Div: during the afternoon the G.O.C motored to the H. Qrs of the 3rd Corps and afterwards to ascertain the situation in our front. General situation unchanged — No operation orders.	BMc

Copy No.

1st ARMY CORPS OPERATION ORDER No. 6.

1st September, 1914.

The 1st Corps will continue its march tomorrow at ~~3 a.m.~~ 2 am and will move towards MEAUX.
    1st Division moving by the main road and using any others to the east for flank guard.
    2nd Division by the roads BETZ - ACY EN MULTIEN - VINCY MANOEUVRE - TREPILLY - BARCY - MEAUX STATION by the right bank of the River MARNE to the bridge at ESBLY.
    3rd Cavalry Brigade to cover the rear and eastern flank.
    5th Cavalry Brigade to cover the rear and western flank.

    All vehicles that are not required in the fighting line must be sent away tonight (at 10 pm) to cross the MARNE at ~~MEAUX~~.

    ~~Before moving off~~ *as it moves* the 2nd Division will place a force of two battalions and a battery on the high ground south of VINCY MANOEUVRE. These troops will remain in position until the others have passed through.
    The 1st Division will place similar forces to cover the road about VARMFROY and in a suitable position near LE PLESSIS PLACY.

    The 3rd Division halts tonight in area VILLERS BOUILLANCY - BREGY - CHEVREVILLE: outposts just west of MACQUETNES to cross-roads west of BOISY.
    3rd Cavalry Brigade will get into touch with 3rd Division as early as possible tomorrow morning and send patrols towards LEVIGNEN.

    Reports to road junction S.E. of LE PLESSIS PLACY after 3 a.m.

                             J.E. GOUGH. Brig. General.
                               S.G.S.O., 1st Army Corps.

Issued at 7 p.m.

Copies to :-
  1st Division
  2nd Division
  3rd Cavalry Brigade
  5th Cavalry Brigade
  O.C. Signals.
  A.D.C. for G.O.C.
  S.G.S.O.
  G.S.O. (1).
  D.A. & Q.M.G.
  A. & Q. Office.
  Camp Commandant.
  War Diary.
  Office.

The Transport of 3rd Cav Bde will precede that of the 2nd Division — that of the 5th Cav Bde will precede that of the 1st Divn

Note:- The 4th Division has captured 8 German guns.
No civilian transport is to be allowed to move on the roads allotted to 1st Corps but must be pushed off Eastwards

MESSAGES AND SIGNALS.

Prefix...Code...m	Words	Charge	This message is on a/c of:	Reed. at...m
Office of Origin and Service Instructions.	Sent			Date
	At...m		...Service.	From
	To			
	By		(Signature of "Franking Officer.")	By

TO: 3rd Bde Operation Order No 11
VILLENOY
2/9/14

Sender's Number | Day of Month | In reply to Number | AAA

1) The English Army move [illegible] in a [illegible]
[illegible] direction to our in touch with the [illegible]
1st Corps — starts at 4 a.m.

2) The rest of the Cavalry is to cover the
movement on our left from the
[illegible]

3) [illegible]

4) [illegible]

5) The Red [illegible] of [illegible] [illegible] under the
Senior [illegible] [illegible] at [illegible] (ESSEX)

From: [illegible] R MARKS OF ISLEY [illegible] VILLENOY
Place:
Time:

The above may be forwarded as now corrected. (Z)

Censor. Signature of Addressor or person authorised to telegraph in his name.
* This line should be erased if not required.

"A" Form. [illegible]

MESSAGES AND SIGNALS.

No. of Message

Prefix .... Code .... m.	Words	Charge	This message is on a/c of:	Recd. at .... m.
Office of Origin and Service Instructions.	Sent		.... Service.	Date
	At .... m.			From
	To			
	By		(Signature of "Franking Officer.")	By

TO

Sender's Number	Day of Month	In reply to Number	AAA
*			

Reporting to the OC Ammunition Column at [illegible]

5. On the arrival of the [illegible] the OC Amm. Col. will march with the [illegible] Ambulances and batteries to [illegible] [illegible] and [illegible] [illegible] [illegible] [illegible]

6. Reports to head of Main Body.

Passed at 11.15 pm

[illegible] Maj. [illegible]

From

Place

Time

The above may be forwarded as now corrected. (Z)

Censor. Signature of Addressor or person authorised to telegraph in his name.

* This line should be erased if not required.

Copy No. 7

1st ARMY CORPS OPERATION ORDER No. 7.

2nd September, 1914.

The British Expeditionary Force was today concentrated on a line ETREPILLY to DAMMARTIN and to the south.

Tomorrow it will move in a south-easterly direction to get into touch with the French 18th Corps.

1st Corps will move at 4 a.m. as follows :-
1st Division, S.P., bridge over River MARNE at VARREDDES by BOIS DE MEAUX and the main road to LA FERTE.
2nd Division, S.P., bridge over MARNE at MEAUX STATION - TRILPORT - MONTCEAUX - FORET DU MANS - SIGNY SIGNETS.
The cavalry will cover the movement from any interference from the north and observe the country about COCHEREL.
Army Troops follow the 2nd Division.
All vehicles not required in the fighting line to move not later than 2 a.m. to the neighbourhood of AULNOY as follows :-
5th Cavalry Brigade by FORET DU MANS - PIERRE LEVEE - AULNOY.
3rd Cavalry Brigade, S.T., bridge over MARNE at MEAUX, 1:30 a.m., by VAUCOURTOIS - COULOMMIERS - AULNOY.
1st Division, S.P., bridge over MARNE at MEAUX and follow 3rd Cavalry Brigade.
2nd Division moving at 2 a.m. by CRECY to COULOMMIERS.
Army Troops follow the 1st Division.

Reports to MEAUX till 6:30 a.m., afterwards to MONTCEAUX.

J.E. GOUGH. Brig. General.
S.G.S.O., 1st Army Corps

Issued at 10:30 p.m.

Copies to :-
1st Division
2nd Division
3rd Cavalry Brigade
5th Cavalry Brigade
O.C. Signals.
A.D.C. for G.O.C.
S.G.S.O.
G.S.O. (1)
D.A. & Q.M.G.
A. & Q. Office
Camp Commandant
War Diary
Office

1) Enemy is moving S.E. from Coulommiers. He is opposed by the 5th French Army.

Our army moves to a position facing N.E., with a view to attacking the enemy.

The 6th French Army is advancing S.E. through MEAUX.

1st Corps – Right on Chapelle Iger } by 9 am
           Left on Lumigny
2nd Corps – Right on La Trousaye
           Left about Vieil Maison } by 10 am
3rd Corps – in neighbourhood of BAILLY by 10 am

The 5th Cav Bde is placed under the orders of the GOC 3rd Cav Bde.

2. The task of the 3rd & 5th Cavalry Brigades is to cover the 2 Corps and to reconnoitre to the North and North East.

3. In consequence the 3rd & 5th Cav Bdes will move independently to points in readiness as follows, to be in position by 10 am.
   3rd Cav Bde – LA BALTHAZERIE Farm (just West of LUMIGNY).
   5th Cav Bde – just West of the Chateau de LUMIGNY, just North of the Road to Tournan, where they will rest and continue their shoeing.

4. The following two Contact Squadrons will be found by the 3rd Cav Bde. (Special instructions have been given to Squadron COs.) at 8.30 am
   ① La Houssaye to Dammartin
   ② R.W. Iverardi to Farehoudres

The 5th Cav Bde will occupy PEZARCHES with a Regiment which will push recce connaissances towards MORPERTHUIS and East on ①A BOUVERE ① through TAVQUIN, ② on MAUPERTHUIS – a ② through the forest of MILSNOISINE & FARVACHE.

MESSAGES AND SIGNALS. Army Form C.2121

5. 'A' Echelon will accompany Brigades 'B' Echelon & L.T. - Amm. Col. and Field Ambulances ~~for Ottens~~ will leave billeting areas at 10 am and march 3rd Brigade to MARIS1 - 5th Brigade to FONTENOY and back clear of the road
2 Light Field Ambulances will accompany each brigade.

6. Reports to PEZARCHES after 8.30 am

Reference attached.
(1) The Brigade will march at 9 am under Col Brooks in the following order 4th Hussars - Bde Bd RHA 2 Light Ambulances - 5th Lancers - 16th Lancers - A Sqdn Route S.P. Cross Roads between RICHEBOURG FARM and QUETCHAIN

(2) Captain H. L. Jennings 5th Lancers will command 'A' Echelon

Copy No. 15

OPERATION ORDER NO. 17

by

Field-Marshal Sir John French, G.C.B., etc.,
Commanding British Expeditionary Force.

General Head Quarters,
5th September 1914.

1. The enemy has apparently abandoned the idea of advancing on PARIS and is contracting his front and moving south-eastward.

2. The Army will advance eastward with a view to attacking.

Its left will be covered by the 6th French Army also marching east and its right will be linked to the 5th French Army marching north.

3. In pursuance of the above, the following moves will take place, the Army facing east on completion of the movement:-

1st Corps (Right on LA CHAPELLE-IGER
(Left on LUMIGNY.

Movement to be completed by 9.a.m.

2nd

Second sheet.

2nd Corps (Right on LA HOUSSAYE
(Left in neighbourhood of VILLENEUVE.

Movement to be completed by 10 a.m.

3rd Corps facing east in neighbourhood of BAILLY.

Movement to be completed by 10 a.m.

Cavalry.

(1) Cavalry Division to guard the front and flank of 1st Corps on the line JOUY LE CHATEL (connecting with V French Army) - COULOMMIERS (connecting with 3rd and 5th Cavalry Brigades).

(2) 3rd and 5th Cavalry Brigades will cease to be under the orders of 1st Corps and will act in concert under instructions issued by Brigadier-General H. Gough. They will cover the 2nd Corps connecting with Cavalry Division on the right and with French VI Army on the left.

4. Trains south of railway NANGIS - VERNEUIL L'ETAING - OZOIR.

4. Roads allotted:-

    1st Corps. GUIGNES - CHAUMES - FONTENAY - MARLES - LUMIGNY inclusive and all roads to E.

    2nd Corps. COUBERT - TOURNAN - VILLENEUVE LE COMTE inclusive and all roads between this and 1st Corps.

    3rd Corps. All roads W. of 2nd Corps.

5. Railheads for 6th September 1914:-

Cavalry Division	MELUN
5th Cavalry Brigade	do.
G.H.Q.	do.

L. of C.

3rd Sheet.

   L. of C.   MELUN

   1st Corps   LIEUSAINT

   2nd Corps   do.

   3rd Corps   BRUNOY

   R.F.C.   do.

   Ammunition Railhead VILLENEUVE ST GEORGES
              (Goods Station).

6. G.H.Q. remains at MELUN.

   Reports centre G.H.Q. TOURNAN from 8 a.m.

            (Sd.) A.J.MURRAY, Lieut.-Genl.,

Issued at 5.30 p.m.   Chief of the General Staff.

Copy No.

Operation / Routine Order No. 2.

By Br Genl Gough cc
MAZAGRAN
Reference MEAUX sheet. 7/9/14

1(b). During today the enemy's forces in our front have been retreating Northwards all along the line.
On our right the French 5th Army are pursuing the German Corps to the line of the Petit Morin, after inflicting severe losses upon them, especially about MONT-CEAUX.
In our front the enemy's retreat has been covered by his 2nd and 9th Cavalry Divs who have suffered severely.
On our left flank two hostile Corps that were withdrawing Northwards across the MARNE, have been heavily attacked by the French 6th Army on the line of the OURCQ.

(1) Our Army continues the pursuit tomorrow in the direction of the MARNE, with its ~~its right of the line~~ on NOGENT, attacking the enemy wherever met.   Roads.
1st Corps ① ST REMY — REBAIS — LA TRETOIRE — BOITRON — LA NOUE CHARLY and ② SABLONNIÈRES — HONDEVILLIERS — NOGENT L'ARTAUD both inclusive. Roads east of this will be used by the French.

Copy No. 27

Operation } Order No.
Routine }

Reference

1(a) 2nd Corps. The road BOISSY LE CHATEL
 — DOUE — ST CYR — SANCY and
 all between this and 1st Corps.
 3rd Corps on JOUARRE, using roads
 west of the 2nd Corps.
 Heads of columns will cross the line
 ST REMY — BOISSY LE CHATEL — LA
 HAUTE MAISON at 6am.

(c) The Cavalry Division and 3rd & 5th Cav
 Brigades will continue the pursuit;
 keeping touch on the right with the Corps
 of Cavalry of the 5th French Army.

2. The first task of the 3rd & 5th Cav Bdes
 will be to reconnoitre and if possible
 to seize the passages of the PETIT MORIN.

3. In consequence
 The 5th Cav Bde will send out at 4.30am
 a Contact Squadron to reconnoitre the
 front LA TRETOIRE — ST OUEN
 The 3rd Cav Bde will send out at 4.30am
 a Contact Squadron moving through
 LES MARCHES on MAUROY and
 reconnoitering LES NEUILLIS — ST CYR
 — LES LOUVIERES.

Copy No. 29

Operation ⎫
Routine ⎬ Order No.
         ⎭

Reference

4. The advanced Guards of both Brigades will march at 5-30 am.
5th Cav Bde marching on CHAMPLION in order to cross the PETIT MORIN about ORLY and ST OUEN.
3rd Cav: Bde marching via LES MARCHES - MAUROY on ST CYR
If both brigades succeed in crossing the River they will establish themselves on the Northern Bank — the 5th Cav: Bde S.W of BUSSIERES, the 3rd Cav Bde at CHAMP TORTEL, when orders for a further advance will be issued.

5 Railhead for Sep 8th CHAULNES.

6 Reports to head of 3rd Cav: Bde

Issued at 11·55 pm

R.H. Kearsley Maj
BM
3 CB.

Gen Gough

SECRET.   Copy No. 2

OPERATION ORDER NO. 18
by
Field-Marshal Sir John French, G.C.B., etc.,
Commanding British Expeditionary Force.

G.H.Q.,
7th September 1914.

1. During today the enemy's forces in our front have been retreating towards the north all along the line.

On our right the French 5th Army are pursuing the German Corps to the line of the PETIT MORIN, after inflicting severe losses upon them, especially about MONTCEAUX which was carried at the point of the bayonet.

In our front the enemy's retreat has been covered by his 2nd and 9th Cavalry Divisions who have suffered severely.

On our left flank two hostile corps, that were withdrawing northwards across the MARNE, have been heavily attacked by the French 6th Army on the line of the OURCQ.

2. The intention of the Field-Marshal Commanding-in-Chief is to continue the pursuit in the direction of the MARNE, with the right of the Army on NOGENT, attacking the enemy wherever met.

3. Roads are allotted as follows:-

<u>1st Corps</u>.   The road ST REMY - REBAIS (eastern road) - LA TRETOIRE - BOITRON - LA NOUE - PAVANT - CHARLY to BREUIL - SABLONNIERES - HONDEVILLIERS - NOGENT L'ARTAUD road inclusive. Roads east of this will be used by the French.

<u>2nd Corps</u>.   The road BOISSY LE CHATEL - DOUE - ST CYR - SAACY and all between this and 1st Corps.

<u>3rd Corps</u>; will march on JOUARRE, using roads west of 2nd Corps.

Heads of Columns will cross the line ST REMY - BOISSY LE CHATEL - LA HAUTE MAISON at 6 a.m.

The Cavalry Division and 3rd and 5th Cavalry Brigades will continue the pursuit, keeping touch on the right with the Corps of Cavalry of the 5th French Army, and on the left with the 6th French Army.

4.

NO. O.B./ B485

Second sheet.

4. Supply railheads for 8th September 1914:-

    Cavalry Division . . . . CHAUMES
    5th Cavalry Brigade . . . . do.
    1st Corps . . . . do.
    G.H.Q. . . . . do.
    L. of C. Units . . . . do.
    Royal Flying Corps . . . . do.
    2nd Corps . . . . MARLES
    3rd Corps . . . . TOURNAN
    Ammunition Railhead . . . . VERNEUIL

5. Reports to MELUN.

                                                   (sd.) Henry Wilson.

Issued at   Lieutenant-General,

                                                                 C.G.S.

"A" Form. Army Form C-2?
MESSAGES AND SIGNALS.

Prefix......Code.......m	Words	Charge	This message is on a/c of:	Recd. at..........m
Office of Origin and Service Instructions.				Date
	Sent			From
	At........................m.		...................Service.	
	To			
	By		(Signature of "Franking Officer.")	By

TO	Orders by Brigadier General H Gough CB
	Cmdg 3 & 5th Cav Bdes
	GRAND M. MENARD 9/9/14

| Sender's Number | Day of Month | In reply to Number | AAA |

1). The outposts of the 2nd Corps are along the COUPRU - MONTREUIL Road - the Roads at FERTÉ PARIS being the junction between the 1st and 2nd Corps. The 5th Cavalry Brigade is at LA BAUVYERE (1½ miles South of COUPRU)

2). The task of the 3rd and 5th Cavalry Brigades is to reconnoitre to the North.

3) In consequence the 5th Cavalry Brigade will send out the following officers patrols at 4 am tomorrow.
① through LA VOIE DUCHATEL on BUSSIARES
② through MARIGNY on VEUILLY
③ on GERMIGNY
④ through SABLONNIERE on DHUISSY

and at 6 am will be in a position of readiness about LA PETITE BOULLOYE (S.E of MARIGNY).

From	
Place	
Time	

The above may be forwarded as now corrected. (Z)

Censor.   Signature of Addressor or person authorised to telegraph in his name
* This line should be erased if not required.

"A" Form.　　　　　　　　　　　　　　　　Army Form C. 212
　　　　　　MESSAGES AND SIGNALS.　　　No. of Message_____

Prefix	Code	m	Words	Charge	This message is on a/c of:	Recd. at	m
Office of Origin and Service Instructions.			Sent			Date	
			At	m	Service.	From	
			To			By	
			By		(Signature of "Franking Officer.")		

TO _____

| Sender's Number | Day of Month | In reply to Number | AAA |

4) The 3rd Cav Bde will march to a position of readiness about LA PLATRIERE (2 miles S.S.W. of MARIGNY). Route SAACY — along road to CITRY — NANTEUIL — MENBROLON — MONTREGNY — PLATRIERES — BEZU LE GUERY — YENTELET FARM — Point 220 LESONGE. Starting Point. Road junction R of PETIT ME MENARD at 4.45 am.

Order of march. (Peace at first).
H.Q — 4th Hussars — 5th Lancers — 3rd Bde RHA — 16th Lancers. 'A' Echelon 1st Line Transport.
Light Ambulances will follow the 3rd Bde RHA.

5) The Ammunition Column — 2nd Cav Field Amb. and 'B' Echelon - 1st Line Transport, will remain at ROUGEVILLE until further orders.

6) Reports to head of 3rd Cav: Bde

From: Issued at 9 pm.　　　　　　R H Crawley Maj Bm
Place　　　　　　　　　　　　　　　　　　　3 CB.
Time

SECRET.

Copy No. 2

OPERATION ORDER NO. 19

by

Field-Marshal Sir John French, G.C.B., etc.,
Commanding British Expeditionary Force.

General Head Quarters,
8th September 1914.

1. The enemy are continuing their retreat northwards and our Army has been successfully engaged during the day with their rear-guards on the PETIT MORIN thereby materially assisting the progress of the French Armies on our right and left, which the enemy have been making great efforts to oppose.

2. The Army will continue the advance north tomorrow at 5 a.m. attacking rear-guards of the enemy wherever met.
    The Cavalry Division will act in close association with the 1st Corps and gain touch with the 5th French Army on the right.
    General Gough, with the 3rd and 5th Cavalry Brigades will act in close association with the 2nd Corps and gain touch with the 6th French Army on the left.

3. Roads are allotted as follows:-

    <u>1st Corps.</u>   Eastern road - SABLONNIERES - HONDEVILLIERS - NOGENT L'ARTAUD - SAULCHERY - Eastern side of CHARLY - LE THALET.
    Western road - LA TRETOIRE - BOITRON - PAVANT - Western side of CHARLY - VILLIERS SUR MARNE - DOMPTIN - COUPRU; both inclusive.

    <u>2nd Corps.</u>   Western road - ST OUEN - SAACY - MNERY - MONTREUIL inclusive and all roads between this and Western road of 1st Corps exclusive.

    <u>3rd Corps.</u>   Western road - LA FERTE SOUS JOUARRE - DHUISY inclusive and all roads between this and Western road of 2nd Corps exclusive.

4. Supply railheads for 9th September 1914;-

Cavalry Division	CHAUMES
Brigadier-Genl. Gough's Command	do.
1st Corps	do.
2nd Corps	COULOMMIERS
3rd Corps	do.
L. of C.	MONTCERF
G.H.Q.	CHAUMES
R.F.C.	do.
Ammunition railhead	VERNEUIL.

5.

Gen. Gough

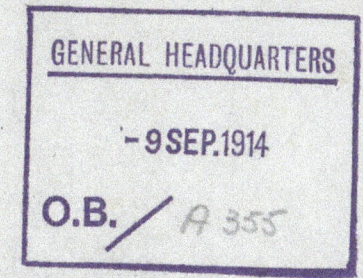

GENERAL HEADQUARTERS
- 9 SEP. 1914
O.B./ A 355

SECRET.   Copy No. 2

OPERATION ORDER NO. 20
by
Field-Marshal Sir John French, G.C.B., etc.,
Commanding British Expeditionary Force.

General Head Quarters,
9th September 1914.

1. The Army today forced the passage of the MARNE.
The 1st and 2nd Corps have reached the line LE THIALET - MONTREUIL.
3rd Corps, opposed by the enemy's Guard and 2nd Cavalry Divisions, holds the north bank of the River at LA FERTE.
During the pursuit the enemy suffered heavy loss in killed and wounded; some hundreds of prisoners have fallen into our hands, and a battery of eight machine guns was captured by 2nd Division.
The 6th French Army has been heavily engaged today along the line CREGY - MARCILLY - PUISIEUX - BOUILLANCY - BETZ, and has successfully resisted all attacks.
The left of the 5th French Army was expected to reach CHATEAU THIERRY this evening.

2. The Army will continue the pursuit northwards tomorrow at 5 a.m. and attack the enemy wherever met.

3. The 3rd Corps will bridge the MARNE during the night so that the Corps may be in a position to cross at 5 a.m., and march on COCHEREL, maintaining touch with the French Cavalry Brigade on its left.
The Cavalry Division will act in close association with 1st Corps and gain touch with 5th French Army on the right.
General Gough, with 3rd and 5th Cavalry Brigades, will act in close association with 2nd Corps and keep touch between 2nd and 3rd Corps.

4. Roads allotted:-

   1st Corps. Eastern Road. LE THALET - LUCY LE BOCAGE - TORCY - PRIEZ - NEUILLY ST FRONT.
   Western Road. COUPRU - MARIGNY EN ORTOIS - BUSSIARES - HAUTE VESNES - ST GENGOULPH - MONNES - PASSY EN VALOIS - NOROY SUR OURCQ, both roads inclusive.

   2nd Corps. Western Road. MONTREUIL - DHUISY - GERMIGNY - SOUS COULOMBS - BRUMETZ - ST QUENTIN - LA FERTE MILON, inclusive, and all roads between this and WESTERN road of 1st Corps, exclusive.

   3rd Corps. Roads West of those allotted to 2nd Corps.

The

Second sheet.

5.   Reports to MELUN till 9 a.m., after that hour to COULOMMIERS.

Issued at   (Sd)   Lieutenant-General,
         7.30pm   Chief of the General Staff.

2nd sheet.

The Cav. Div. Transport and Supply Columns will use the eastern road allotted to the 1st Corps.
The 2nd Corps will arrange with General Gough regarding the road to be used by the transport of the 3rd and 5th Brigades.

5. Supply Railheads for 10/9/14:-

    Cavalry Division   JOUY SUR MORIN
    1st Corps   ST SIMEON
    2nd Corps   CHAILLY-BOISSY
    Gen:Gough's Command   COULOMMIERS
    3rd Corps   -do-
    L. of C.   -do-
    G.H.Q.   -do-
    R.F.C.   -do-
    Ammunition Railhead   VERNEUIL

6. Reports to COULOMMIERS.

Issued at 8.15 p.m.

(Sd.) HENRY WILSON, for

Lieutenant-General,
C.G.S.

Copy No. 52

Operation / Routine Order No.

Reference 5' [?]
          16 [Lancers]
          M A Battery
          Ammn Column
          R [Royal] [?]
          B [?]

(1) Reference attached Operation Order
No 5. In order of march 4th 3rd Cav
Bde will be:-
          16 Lancers + 5 Lancers -
          R.H.A. + Hussars - A Echelon

(2) The Ammn Column and 2 Cav Fd Amb.
and B and [?] [?] will march at
10·30 am via WETHERLY ST FRONT
to BILLY BURROUGHS ([?] [?] [?])

"A" Form.   Army Form C. 2121.

MESSAGES AND SIGNALS.

TO: Operation Orders Number 5
by Brig Gen H Gough CB
MAR 17th   11.9.14

1(a.) During the advance yesterday seven guns many machine guns well over 1000 prisoners and much transport have fallen into our hands. The enemy left many dead on the field.

(b.) The army continues the pursuit in a North Easterly direction at 5am and crossing the OURCQ will reach the line BRUYERES—CUGNY—STREMY—LALOGE FERME north of CHOUY.

2. The task of the 3rd and 5th Cav Bde is to press the enemy reconnoitring for our and third Corps

"A" Form.
MESSAGES AND SIGNALS.
Army Form C. 2121.

3. In consequence the following officers patrols will be sent out at 5 am.
(1) By 3rd Cav Bde (16th Lancers) via CHOUY VILLERS HELON, VIERZY on BERZY
(2) by 5th Cav Bde via STE REMY, PARCY TIGNY - BUZANCY.
(3) By 5th Cav Bde via BILLY SUR OURCQ - LE PLESSIER HULEU, HARTENNES DROISY - AMBRIEF.
The patrols will report first contact with the enemy & negative or other information from the above named places. Report to CHOUY till 8.30 am after that hour via STE REMY

4. The Bdes will march from their billets at 6 am. 3rd Bde on NOROY the 5th Bde on CHOUY. The exact line of advance of Bdes will be as follows

"A" Form.   Army Form C. 21[?]
MESSAGES AND SIGNALS.   No. of Message_____

Prefix____ Code____ m	Words	Charge	This message is on a/c of:	Recd. at_____ m
Office of Origin and Service Instructions.				Date
_____	Sent		_____Service.	From
_____	At_____m.			
_____	To			
_____	By		(Signature of "Franking Officer.")	By

TO {

| Sender's Number | Day of Month | In reply to Number | AAA |

3rd Cav Bde STREMY. BLANZY. TIGNY.
5th Cav Bde BILLY sur OURCQ LE PLESSIER HULEU. HARTENNES DROIZY
5. The 2nd Corps has been ordered to arrange for the forwarding of the transport of 3rd and 5th Cav Bdes
6. Railhead COULOMMIERS
7. The French 6th Army are using the LAFERTE MILON. TROESNES LONGPONT road.
8. Reports K. heap of 3rd Cav Bde Innes at 2.10 a.m.

R H Kearsley Maj
3 CB

From
Place
Time
The above may be forwarded as now corrected. (Z)
        Censor.   Signature of Addressee or person authorised to telegraph in his name
* This line should be erased if not required.

Wt. W1154/2240. 7/11. 7,500,000. Sch. 4a. "A" Form. Army Form C. 2121.

MESSAGES AND SIGNALS.

Prefix	Code	m.	Words	Charge	This message is on a/c of:	Recd. at	m.
Office of Origin and Service Instructions.			Sent		Service.	Date	
			At	m.		From	
			To			By	
			By		(Signature of "Franking Officer.")		

TO Operation Orders Number 5
    by Brig Gen H. Gough CB
MARTY   11.9.14

Sender's Number. | Day of Month. | In reply to Number

AAA

a.) During the advance yesterday seven guns many machine guns well over 1000 prisoners and much transport have fallen into our hands. The enemy left many dead on the field.

b.) The army continues the pursuit in a North Easterly direction at 5am and crossing the OURCQ will reach the line BRUYERES - CUGNY - St REMY - LALOGE FERME North of CHOUY

The task of the 3rd and 5th Cav Bde is to pursue the enemy reconnoitring for our 2nd and third Corps

From
Place
Time

The above may be forwarded as now corrected. (Z)

Censor. Signature of Addressor or person authorised to telegraph in his name.
* This line should be erased if not required.

"A" Form.　　　　　　　　　　　　　　Army Form
MESSAGES AND SIGNALS.　　　　No. of Message_____

Prefix_____ Code_____ m	Words	Charge	This message is on a/c of:	Recd. at_____ m
Office of Origin and Service Instructions	Sent			Date_____
_____	At_____ m		_____ Service.	From_____
_____	To_____		(Signature of "Franking Officer.")	By_____
	By_____			

TO { | | | | | }

Sender's Number	Day of Month	In reply to Number	AAA
	3rd Cav Bde ST REMY. BLANZY. TIGNY.		
	5th Cav Bde BILLY SUR OURCQ LE PLESSIER HULEU. HARTENNES DROISY		
	5. The 2nd Corps has been ordered to arrange for the forwarding of the transport of 3rd and 5th Cav Bdes		
	6. Railhead COULOMMIERS.		
	7. The French 6th Army are using the LAFERTE MELUN, TROESNES LONGPONT roads		
	8. Report head of 3rd Cav Bde arrives at 2.15 am		
		A.D. Kearsley Maj GSO	
		30/9	

From_____
Place_____
Time_____

The above may be forwarded as now corrected.　(Z)

Censor.　　Signature of Addressor or person authorised to telegraph in his name

* This line should be erased if not required.

MESSAGES AND SIGNALS.

Prefix	Code	m.	Words	Charge	This message is on a/c of:	Recd. at _____ m.
Office of Origin and Service Instructions.			Sent At _____ m. To By _____		_____ Service. (Signature of "Franking Officer.")	Date _____ From _____ By _____

TO

Sender's Number	Day of Month	In reply to Number	AAA

3. In consequence the following officers patrols will be sent out at 3 a.m.
(1) By ... (3rd/11th Lancers) via CHOUY VILLERS HELON VIERZY & SERZY
(2) by 5th Cav Bde via Ste REMY, PAR CYTIGNY - BUZANCY.
(3) By 3rd Cav Bde via BILLY SUR OURCQ - LE PLESSIER HELEU HARTENNES DROISY & AMBRIEF.
The patrols will report just contact with the enemy & whatever other information from the above named places. Report to CHOUY till 8.30 am. After that hour via Ste REMY.

4. The Bdes will march from their billets at 6 a.m. 3rd Bde on NOROY the 5th on CHOUY the [line?] of advance of Bdes will be as follows.

From _____
Place _____
Time _____

The above may be forwarded as now corrected. (Z)
Censor. Signature of Addresser or person authorised to telegraph in his name.
* This line should be erased if not required.

SECRET.   Copy No. 2

OPERATION ORDER NO. 21
by
Field-Marshal Sir John French, G.C.B., etc.,
Commanding British Expeditionary Force.

Gen Gough

General Head Quarters,
10th September 1914.

1. During the advance today the 1st and 2nd Corps have been opposed by strong rearguards of all arms, and assisted by the Cavalry Division on the right, 3rd and 5th Cavalry Brigades on the left, have driven the enemy northwards. Seven guns, many machine guns, well over 1,000 prisoners and much transport have fallen into our hands. The enemy left many dead on the field.

2. The Army will continue the pursuit in a north-easterly direction tomorrow at 5 a.m., and crossing the OURCQ will reach the line BRUYERES - CUGNY - ST REMY - LA LOGEFERME (north of CHOUY).
   The Cavalry Division and General Gough's Command will carry out the same role as today.

3. Roads will be allotted as follows:-

   1st Corps.
      Eastern Road.   MONTHIERS - GRISOLLES - ROCOURT ST MARTIN - FERE EN TARDENOIS (inclusive).
      Western Road.   PRIEZ - LATILLY - OULCHY LE CHATEAU - BEUGNEUX (inclusive).
   2nd Corps.
      Western Road.* PASSY EN VALOIS - MONTRON - NEUILLY ST FRONT - VICHEL VAUTEUIL - BILLY SUR OURCQ - ST REMY - HARTENNES (inclusive), and all roads between this and the Western road of the 1st Corps.

   3rd Corps.   Roads between Western road of 2nd Corps (exclusive) and the road LA FERTE MILON - TROESNES - LONGPONT (exclusive), the latter being used by the French 6th Army. The 3rd Corps will arrange with the 2nd Corps for the use of the road BRUMETZ - CHEZY EN ORXOIS - PASSY EN VALOIS - CHOUY which will be cleared by the 2nd Corps as early as possible.

4. The Cavalry Division transport and supply columns will use the Eastern road allotted to the 1st Corps.
   The 2nd Corps will arrange with General Gough regarding the road to be used by the transport of the 3rd and 5th Cavalry Brigades.

5. Railheads for September 11th will be the same as for today.

6. Reports to COULOMMIERS.

                                              (sd) A. Murray
                                              Lieutenant-General,
                                              C.G.S.

Issued at 8/15 p.m.

* The road DAMMARD - NEUILLY ST FRONT and all roads to the West will be cleared by the 1st Corps by 8 a.m.

Operation order no 7

11 Sept 1914
B. 924

1. our army was halted last night
in close touch with the 6th French army
on our left and the 5th French army
on our right.

(2) our army continues the pursuit today
at 5am & Heads of Corps to reach the
line LIERVAL - CHAVIGNON - TERNY
Roads are allotted as follows.
1st Corps Eastern Road LONGUEVAL -
BOURG - CHAMOUILLE - BRUYERES -
ATHIES - Western Road
BRAINE. PRESLES. CHAVONNE.
LIERVAL. PRESLES. LAON
2nd Corps western Road. CH'ACRISE
- MISSY. AISNE. VREGNY. PONT RO-
UGE. BASCULE. PINON - ANIZY LE
CHATEAU SUZY.
3rd Corps COURMELLES - SOISSONS
TERNY - COUCY LE CHATEAU ST G-OBAI-
N.
Cav Div uses the Eastern Road
allotted to the 1st Corps.

2. The role of the 3rd Cav Div is to continue
the pursuit northward. Further
orders as to direction will be
known what bridges over the AISNE

"A" Form.   Army Form C. 2121.
MESSAGES AND SIGNALS.   No. of Message

3. In consequence patrols have to
be sent out by the 3rd Cav Bde to reconnoitre
the bridges at VAILLY and CONDÉ.
The 5th Cav Bde will march to a
position of readiness South of
CHASSEMY.
The 3rd Cav Bde will remain in its billets
ready to saddle up at a moments
notice.

4. All transport will be parked clear
of the road and will follow in rear
of the fighting troops of the 2nd Corps
in front of that Corps' transport.

5. Supply Columns will refill from the
Reserve parks on the main road between
LATILLY and NEUILLY ST FRONT.
Ammunition park will replenish at
NOGENT L'ARTAUD as early as
possible.

6. Reports to CHATEAU CHASSEMY.
Issued at 5.40 am.

R H Kearsley Major
BM
3CB.

Copy No. 6

2nd Army Corps

OPERATION ORDER No.23.

Reference Map   Headquarters, 2nd Army Corps,
                                    13th
                                    ~~14th~~ September, 1914.

1. The retreat of the German forces in our front has continued during the day, and the enemy's disorganization appears to be increasing. The enemy's 2nd, 3rd and 4th (Reserve) Corps appear to be in our front and are being reinforced by the 25th Landwehr Division, which is being hurriedly withdrawn from Belgium for this purpose.

    Our 3rd Division captured a hundred prisoners and a machine gun and team in BRAINE.

    The Army is halted to-night in close touch with the French 6th Army on our left and 5th Army on our right.

2. The Army will continue the pursuit today at 7 a.m. Heads of Corps will reach the line LIERVAL - CHAVIGNON - TERNY.

3. Second Corps will reach the line CHAVIGNON - VAUDESSON ~~/XXXXXXX/~~. Main bodies starting at 7 a.m. except for any operations conducted by Fifth Division before that hour against MISSY SUR AISNE.

4. The following roads are allotted-
    1st Corps Western road BRAINE - PRESLES - CHAVONNE - LIERVAL - PRESLES (two miles S.W. of BRUYERES).
    2nd Corps Western road CHACRISE - MISSY SUR AISNE - VREGNY - PONT ROUGE (one mile N.W. of VREGNY) - BASCULE (three quarter mile East of LAFFAUX) - PINON - ANIZY LE CHATEAU. This road is allotted to Fifth Division.
    The following road is also allotted to Fifth Division:-

page 2

CONDE SUR AISNE - SANCY - VAUDESSON - PONT DU JOUR.

Third Division is allotted all roads between last named road and Western road allotted to First Corps.

In the event of VAILLY bridge being broken or unsuitable for transport CONDE bridge may be used by Third Division.

5. In the event of 3rd and 5th Cavalry Brigades receiving instructions from G.H.Q. to cover the march of the 2nd Corps, 2nd line transport of those Brigades will remain parked clear of the roads until fighting troops of the 2nd Corps have passed. It will then follow in rear but have precedence of 2nd line transport of the Divisions, that of 5th Cavalry Brigade in rear of 5th Division, 3rd Cavalry Brigade in rear of 3rd Division. This will be regulated by 2nd Corps Staff.

6. Supply Columns will draw supplies tomorrow from reserve parks which will be on the road between LATILLY and NEUILLY-ST-FRONT.

Rendezvous for 3rd Division GRAND ROZOY at 1 p.m.
Rendezvous for 5th Division HARTENNES at 1 p.m.
No.5 Ammunition Park is on road just S.E. of HARTENNES.

Replenishing point for ammunition at REGENT L'ABBAIE

7. Corps Headquarters and Corps Troops will be ready to leave MURET at 10 a.m.

8. Reports to CHATEAU MURET until further orders.

(Sd) G.P.WALKER,
Brigadier General, General Staff
2nd Army Corps.

Issued at 1.30 a.m.

SECRET.   Copy No. 5

OPERATION ORDER NO. 23
by
Field-Marshal Sir John French, G.C.B., etc.,
Commanding British Expeditionary Force.

General Head Quarters,
12th September 1914.

1.   The enemy continued retreating today. There was some opposition South of SOISSONS and on the line of the VESLE.
   The Army is halted tonight in close touch with the French 6th Army on our left and 5th Army on our right.

2.   The Army will continue the pursuit tomorrow at seven a.m.

3.   Heads of Corps will reach the line LIERVAL - CHAVIGNON - TERNY.

4.   Roads allotted:-

1st Corps.
   Eastern Road.   LONGUEVAL - BOURG - CHAMOUILLE - BRUYERES - ATHIES (inclusive).
   Western Road.   BRAINE - PRESLES (2 miles south-east of VAILLY) - CHAVONNE - LIERVAL - PRESLES (2 miles south-west of BRUYERES) - LAON (inclusive).

2nd Corps.
   Western Road.   CHACRISE - MISSY SUR AISNE - VREGNY - PONT ROUGE - BASCULE - PINON - ANIZY LE CHATEAU - SUZY (inclusive) and all roads between this and the Western road of the 1st Corps.(exclusive).

3rd Corps.   COURMELLES - SOISSONS - TERNY - COUCY LE CHATEAU - ST GOBAIN (inclusive) and all roads between this and Western road of 2nd Corps.(exclusive).

5.   The Cavalry Division will use the Eastern road allotted to the 1st Corps.
   The 2nd Corps will arrange with General Gough as to the allotment of roads for transport of the 3rd and 5th Cavalry Brigades. Cavalry transport will have precedence over that of Corps.

Second sheet.

6. Supply Columns will fill up on the 13th from Reserve Parks as follows:-

    Cavalry Division   ⎫
    1st Corps   ⎬ Main road between FERE EN TARDENOIS
    R.F.C.   ⎬ and COINCY.
    L. of C. Units.   ⎭

    Genl. Gough's   ⎫
      Command.   ⎬ Main road between LATILLY and NEUILLY
    2nd Corps   ⎭ ST FRONT.

    3rd Corps   Main road between MONNES and
                            LA FERTE MILON at a point about
                            south-west of PASSY.

Ammunition Parks replenish at NOGENT L'ARTAUD and all empty lorries of the Parks should be sent there to replenish as early as can be arranged.

7. Reports to FERE EN TARDENOIS.

(Sd) A.J.Murray.
Lieutenant-General,
Chief of the General Staff.

Issued at 7.45 pm

G.H.Q.
C.1. 13.9.14

The 3ʳᵈ Cav Brig have not yet received their supplies, nor had they any supplies yesterday. The bridge at Vailly is broken and I beleive the bridge at Condé is broken also, but am sending to verify this.

Under these circumstances, I propose to ~~send~~ keep 3ʳᵈ Cav Brig here until it receives its supplies, and the bridges are repaired by the II Corps, as I have no means to do so.

The 5ᵗʰ Cav Brig, should be ready to advance over the Condé — the Vailly, or the Chavonne bridge as soon as they are practicable.

I would be obliged if I could receive definite orders daily (1) as to what places I am to reconnoitre, and what information is required. (2) the axis of march of my Brigades and the time they are expected to reach daily

(3) What distance ahead of the Infantry I am expected to be.

At present I practically receive no orders. In consequence it is impossible to act with decision and without constant hesitation. Every night the Infantry columns come up and crowd us out of billets to the great detriment of the efficiency of our men and horses. This is particularly fatal, if this weather is to continue.

When may I expect my Squadron 16 Lancers at present attached 4th Div'n to be sent back please? There are two Squadrons 19th Hussars here, attached to 5th Division. I trust that one of these may be ordered to relieve the Squadron 16 Lancers today, please.

The 3rd Cav Brigade have not yet received even its "first reinforcements"

and as a matter of fact, much larger
reinforcements are required now.

Haldane.
Bt-General

Chassemy.
5. A.M
13-9-14

"A" Form.
MESSAGES AND SIGNALS. Army Form C. 2121.

| Prefix | Code | m. | Words | Charge | This message is on a/c of: | Recd. at | m. |

Office of Origin and Service Instructions.

Sent At ... m. To ... By ...

TO GENERAL GOUGH

O.B./D533

| Sender's Number | Day of Month | In reply to Number | |
| *OA 908 | 13 | G 1 | AAA |

Your supplies left railhead each day early aaa that you have not received them must be due to difficulty in passing them through roads filled too by our Corps aaa Operation orders of 12th September para 5 and previous dates make provision for the difficulty and the question now depends on the energy of your supply officers aaa As regards your role your orders were to harass the retreating enemy acting on the left of the Cavalry Division in close co-operation with the 2nd Corps aaa It may in certain circumstances be possible to give you a more

From
Place
Time

Wt. W1154/2240. 7/11. 7,500,000. Sch. 4a.   "A" Form.   Army Form C. 2121.
MESSAGES AND SIGNALS.   No. of Message_____

Prefix____Code____m.	Words	Charge	This message is on a/c of:	Recd. at_____m.
Office of Origin and Service Instructions.				Date_____
_____	Sent		_____Service.	From_____
	At_____m.			
_____	To_____			By_____
	By_____		(Signature of "Franking Officer.")	

TO 2nd

| Sender's Number. | Day of Month | In reply to Number | A A A |

definite role but as the
2nd Corps has aeroplanes attached to it it is considered
that advantage can better be
taken by you of the information
thus gained by the GOC 2nd
Corps than by definite orders
issued by G.H.Q. aaa ~~Squadron~~
~~Humans~~ No orders were issued
by G.H.Q that divisional squadrons
should be sent to divisions as soon
as their positions on the line of
march rendered such action
feasible aaa Further orders
will be issued on the subject aaa
Question of first reinforcement
for 3 Cav B'de is being enquired into.

From_____
Place_____
Time_____
The above may be forwarded as now corrected.   (Z)
_____
Censor.   Signature of Addressor or person authorised to telegraph in his name.
* This line should be erased if not required.

MESSAGES AND SIGNALS.

Army Form C. 2121.

TO 3d

Immediately the Squadron of 19th
Hussars reached the 4th Division
your Squadron of 16th Lancers
should rejoin you.

A.J. Murray
Lt Genl
C.G.S.

?? of you ????? about the
condition of your ??

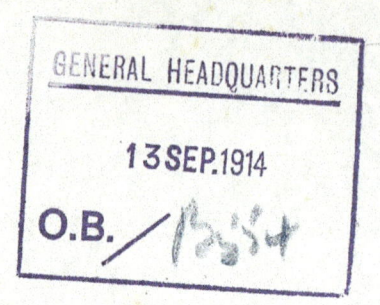

SECRET.   Copy No. 5

OPERATION ORDER NO. 24
by
Field-Marshal Sir John French, G.C.B., etc.,
Commanding British Expeditionary Force.

General Head Quarters,
13th September 1914.

1. The Army has succeeded in obtaining a footing on the North side of the AISNE in face of considerable opposition by strong rearguards of the enemy's 3rd Corps supported by one or two cavalry divisions.
    The 5th and 6th French Armies have also succeeded in crossing on our right and left respectively, working in close touch with us.

2. The Army will continue the pursuit tomorrow at six a.m. and act vigorously against the retreating enemy.

3. Heads of Corps will reach the line LAON - SUZY - FRESNE.

4. Roads allotted:-

1st Corps.

    Eastern Road. BOURG - CHAMOUILLE - BRUYERES - ATHIES inclusive.
    Western Road. PRESLES - CHAVONNE - LIERVAL - LAON inclusive.

2nd Corps.
    Western Road. MISSY SUR AISNE - PONT ROUGE - PINON - ANIZY LE CHATEAU - SUZY inclusive, and all roads between this and Western Road of 1st Corps.

3rd Corps.
    Western Road. VENIZEL - BUCY LE LONG - CROUY - BRAYE - CLAMECY - TERNY - COUCY LE CHATEAU - ST GOBAIN inclusive, and all roads between this and Western Road of 2nd Corps.

5. The Cavalry Division will advance in the general direction COURTECON - LAON.
    Communication must be maintained with 1st Corps.
    General Gough's Command in the general direction ALLEMANT - WISSIGNICOURT.
    Communication must be maintained with 2nd Corps.
    Every effort must be made to harass the enemy's retreat.

6. Arrangements will be made between 1st Corps and Cavalry Division and between 2nd Corps and General Gough's Command, with regard to cavalry billets and roads to be used by cavalry transport and supply columns, which in all cases will have precedence over transport allotted to Corps.

Second sheet.

7. Supply railheads for 14th September will be:-

       1st Cavalry Division   FERE EN TARDENOIS

       1st Corps   do.

       G.H.Q.   do.

       R.F.C.   do.

       L. of C. Units.   do.

       General Gough's Command   OULCHY-BRENY

       2nd Corps   do.

       3rd Corps   NEUILLY ST FRONT

Ammunition Parks will continue to replenish at NOGENT L'ARTAUD.

8. Reports to FERE EN TARDENOIS.

                (Sd.) A.J.MURRAY,
                         Lieutenant-General,
Issued at   Chief of the General Staff.
  6 p.m.

Copy No. **84**

Operation / Routine Order No.

Reference

[handwritten notes, largely illegible]

... 16 ... R.H.A.
... Column ... field ...
... C.R.A. ... Column B echelon

1. ... will assemble at the cross roads of
CHASSEMY at 4 AM ... which of ...
... Park will follow at about 7 am, halting
... Park at VAILLY.

2. ... B echelon will bivouac near the
squares.

3. ... 4
... Park ... bivouac ...

14-4-'14

[signatures illegible]
2nd Cav Bgde

Copy No. 73

Operation / Routine Order No. 8

Reference

To Brig General H.P. Gough
Commanding 2nd Cav. Bde.

CHASSEMY
14-9-14.

1. Our army with the 5th and 6th Armies on our right and left respectively have succeeded in obtaining a footing on the North side of the RIVER AISNE.

The Army continues the pursuit today at 6am, heads of Corps to reach the line LAON – SUZY – FRESNE.

Road are allotted as follows:—
1st Corps:— Eastern Road — BOURG – CHAMOUILLE – BROYETES – ATHIES. Western Road — PRESLES – CHAVONNE – LIERVAL – LAON.

2nd Corps :— Western Road —
MISSY SUR AISNE – PONT ROUGE – PINON – ANIZY LE CHATEAU – SUZY.

3rd Corps — Western Road —
VENIZEL – BUCY LE LONG – LEUILLY – CRAYE – CLAMECY – TERNY – ANIZY LE CHATEAU – ST GOBAIN

The

Copy No. 76

Operation / Routine Order No. 8 (Cont'd)

PAGE - 2.

Reference

1. The 1st Cavalry Divn. advances in the general direction COURTECON-LAON maintaining communication with the 1st Corps.

2. The task of the 2nd Cavy Divn is to harass the enemy's retreat in the general direction ALLEMENT-WISSIGNICOURT maintaining communication with the 2nd Corps.

3. In consequence the 5th Cavy Bgde will assemble in Column of Route with its head at the Canal Bridge at VAILLY at 6. A.M. The 3rd Cavy Bgde will assemble in Column of Route 16th Lancers 4th Hussars 3rd Bgde R.H.A. 5th Lancers A Squadron 16th Lancers with its head at the gate of CHASSEMY CHATEAU at 6.15 A.M.

4. 2nd Corps will make arrangements so as that Billeting parties to be used by the 2nd Cavy Divn transport and supply columns shall will have precedence over transport allotted to the Corps.

Page 3

Copy No. 81

Operation Order No. 8 (cont'd)

5. The supply railhead for September 14th is OULCHY-BRENY. The Ammunition Park will replenish at NOGENT-L'ARTAUD

6. Report to the head of the 3rd Cavalry Brigade.

Issued at 3.55 A.M.

R.M. Yeatsley Major
18th
3 C B

2nd Army Corps

OPERATION ORDER No.24.

Copy No. 1

2nd Army Corps Headquarters,
13th September, 1914.

1. The Army has succeeded in obtaining a footing on the North side of the AISNE in face of considerable opposition by strong rearguards of the enemy's Third Corps, supported by one or two Cavalry Divisions.

   The Fifth and Sixth French Armies have also succeeded in crossing on our right and left respectively, working in close touch with us.

2. The Army will continue the pursuit tomorrow at 6 a.m., and will act vigourously against the retreating enemy.

   Heads of Corps will reach the line LAON - SUZY - FRESNES.

3. 2nd Corps will advance to the line MOLINCHART - SUZY.

4. The following roads are allotted -
   1st Corps Western road PRESLES - CHAVONNE - LIERVAL - LAON inclusive.
   5th Division Western road MISSY SUR AISNE - PONT ROUGE - PINON - ANIZY LE CHATEAU - SUZY inclusive. 5th Division Eastern road SANCY - VAUDESSON - CHAILLEVOIS - EIZY - CESSIERES.
   3rd Division all roads between 1st Corps road (LAON town exclusive) and Eastern 5th Division road.

5. General Gough's Cavalry command has been directed to advance in the general direction ALLEMANT - WISSIGNICOURT. He will arrange with 3rd or 5th Divisional Commander as to whether he crosses by VAILLY bridge or by CONDE or MISSY bridges and will ascertain from them the hour at which those bridges will be free.

Page 2.

6.   Echelon B of Cavalry will follow in rear of fighting troops 2nd Army Corps, but have precedence over the Divisional Trains.

7.   Rendezvous and refilling points 3rd Division just South of BRAINE at 7 a.m.

Rendezvous at refilling point 5th Division cross road ½ mile North of FME DE L'EPITAPHE at 7 a.m.

Supply Columns will then return after evacuating wounded to refill from Reserve Parks on the OULCHY LA VILLE - BRENY road and rendezvous by 3 p.m. on the road just South East of HARTENNES facing North.

8.   No. 3 Ammunition Park will be at cross roads ½ mile North of G in LEGES at 10 a.m. with Section at FME DE L'EPITAPHE.

Replenishing place for ammunition NOGENT L'ARTAUD.

9.   Corps Headquarters and Corps Troops will be ready to start from MURET at 10 a.m.   Route will be given later.

10.   Reports to MURET CHATEAU until further Orders.

(sd) G.F. WALKER,
Brigadier-General, General Staff,
2nd Army Corps.

Issued at 9.50 p.m.

"A" Form. Army Form C. 2121.
MESSAGES AND SIGNALS. No. of Message_____

Prefix____ Code____m.	Words	Charge	This message is on a/c of:	Recd. at____m.
Office of ___ and Service Instructions	Sent			Date____
	At____m.		Service	From____
	To____			
	By____		(Signature of "Franking Officer.")	By____

TO {

| * | Sender's Number | Day of Month | In reply to Number | AAA |

Reference BM1 ... edge of the wood
the ... Cav Bde will assemble near
the mans ... road ... in the hollow
M⁴ de COURSE ... NE of COURCEUX
may ... 3ʳᵈ Cav Bde all assemble near
A ... ENAINE - CROISETTE road just south
of ... the wood at FE du FAUX
... advance ...

the ... Cav B⁴ ... with ... Fd Ambulances
and the ... M̄ Line Transport will
remain at LIMS

Return to the ridge of ... the ...
... road ... S of ...

From____
Place____
Time____

The above may be forwarded as now corrected. (Z) _____
Censor. Signature of Addressee or person authorised to telegraph in his name.
* This line should be erased if not required.

"A" Form.   Army Form C. 2121.
MESSAGES AND SIGNALS.

TO	5th Cav Bde	4th Hussars	3rd Bde R.H.A.	A Echelon
		5th Lancers	Amm. Col.	B Echelon
		16th Lancers	2nd Cav. Fd. Amb	

Sender's Number: BM 1   Day of Month: 15th   AAA

The 2nd Army continues its attack on AIZY at 6 a.m. AAA The 2nd Cav Divn has been asked to cooperate by making a demonstration against CONDE AAA In consequence 1 Squadron 16th Lancers and D and E batteries R.H.A. will assemble at the level crossing 1 mile N.W. of LIME at 5 a.m. Col. BREEKS reporting at 3rd Cav. Bde. Hd Qrs at 3.45 a.m for orders AAA 1 squadron 4th Hussars and the machine guns of the 3rd Cav Bde. under Lt. ROBINSON will assemble at 5 a.m. on the BRAINE - BRENELLE road just clear of BRAINE where the G.O.C. will give them orders AAA The remainder of the 3rd Cav Bde and the whole of the 5th Cav Bde will remain in their billets ready to saddle up at a moments notice.

From: GEN GOUGH   Place: Chateau LIME   Time: 1.45 a.m.

Censor: R H Kearsley Major A.M.

Wt. W1154/2240. 7/11. 7,500,000. Sch. 4a.	"A" Form.		Army Form C. 2121.
	MESSAGES AND SIGNALS.		No. of Message 107

Prefix	Code	m.	Words	Charge	This message is on a/c of:	Recd. at	m.
Office of Origin and Service Instructions.			Sent			Date	
			At	m.	Service.	From	
			To			By	
			By		(Signature of "Franking Officer.")		

TO ~~3rd Cav Bde~~
~~Third and Fifth Divisions and First Corps~~
~~Third Corps~~
Third Cav Bde

Sender's Number.	Day of Month	In reply to Number	
* G119	14th		A A A

It is understood that first Corps is prepared
 with its
~~to advance~~ ~~its~~ left columns with their left on
AIZY to-morrow AAA Third Division it is hoped
will be able to co-operate with this movement
with its right on AIZY AAA If this is correct
as regards ~~first Corps~~ second Corps will be
glad to know time of advance and direction
whence advance will be made AAA Fifth Division
will renew the attack on CHIVRES at daybreak
and Divisional Commander is now arranging for
combined movement for that purpose AAA
Intentions of third Corps not yet known AAA.
There are therefore two separate attacks for

From			
Place			
Time			

The above may be forwarded as now corrected. (Z)

Censor. Signature of Addressor or person authorised to telegraph in his name.

* This line should be erased if not required.

MESSAGES AND SIGNALS.

Page 2.

AAA

which Artillery supporting fire is required AAA
As regards the right attack of which the centre
may be taken as being AIZY it is understood that
the whole of the third Divisional artillery is
available on the left bank of the river but it
is not known to what extent the third Corps
Artillery can assist AAA On the other hand part at
least of the third Divisional artillery should be
able to afford effective support to the attack on
CHIVRES by shelling the GERMAN shelter trenches and
the GERMAN artillery believed to be in the neighbourhood of point 166 AAA It would seem best that
the whole of the fifth Divisional Artillery on the
left bank of the river should be concentrated on

Wt. W1154/2240. 7/11. 7,500,000. Sch. 4a.	"A" Form.	Army Form C. 2121.

MESSAGES AND SIGNALS.

No. of Message_____

Page 3.

AAA

these points and on the plateau due North AAA
In addition to any infantry support which the
third Corps can give to the attack on CHIVRES
it would seem advisable for that Corps to give
the fullest Artillery support that they can
spare to the attack on CHIVRES AAA Third and
fifth Divisions will wire their recommendations
as regards the above general plan and first and
third Corps will oblige by saying how far they
are able to co-operate in the same directions
AAA

From: Second Corps
Place:
Time: P.M.

Wt. W1154/2240. 7/11. 7,500,000. Sch. 4a.   "A" Form.   Army Form C. 2121.

MESSAGES AND SIGNALS.

Page 4

AAA

Third and fifth cavalry brigades can best
co-operate by strong artillery support against
CONDE bridge CELLES and Point 166 as well as
the plateau beyond AAA If this can be supported
by dismounted demonstrations against CONDE
bridge all the better AAA Fifth Divisional
Commander desires that this Artillery support
shall be rendered at five a.m.

From Second Corps
Place
Time 10/10 P.M.

GIFW BG

"A" Form. Army Form C. 2121.
MESSAGES AND SIGNALS. No. of Message_____

Prefix____ Code____m	Words	Charge	This message is on a/c of:	Recd. at____m
Office of Origin and Service Instructions.	Sent			Date
____	At____m		____Service.	From
____	To			By
____	By		(Signature of "Franking Officer.")	

TO { Genl Gough

| Sender's Number | Day of Month | In reply to Number | AAA |
| OA/950 | 14 | | |

concert with II Corps so as to give every assistance tomorrow.

> GENERAL HEADQUARTERS
> P.M. SEP 14 1914
> No. O.B./B 591

From: G.H.Q.
Place:
Time: 10.10 PM

The above may be forwarded as now corrected. (Z) [signature]
Censor. Signature of Addresser or person authorised to telegraph in his name.
* This line should be erased if not required.

S E C R E T

OPERATION ORDER NO. 25
by
Field-Marshal Sir John French, G.C.B., etc.,
Commander-in-Chief, British Forces in the Field.

General Head Quarters,
14th September 1914.

1. The situation as far as known along the whole line from left to right is as follows:-

6th French Army.

The 6th French Army is engaged along the right bank of the AISNE, from SOISSONS to ATTICHY. On the extreme left the 4th Corps was marching with its left on NAMPCEL this afternoon.

3rd Corps.

The 3rd Corps holds the spurs north-west and north-east of BUCY LE LONG having been closely engaged with the enemy all day.

2nd Corps.

The 5th Division is on the line South of S. of CHIVRES - ST MARGUERITE tonight where it has been engaged during the day.

The 3rd Division holds a position from the railway bridge south-east of VAILLY - North of VAILLY - knoll West of VAILLY. It has been heavily engaged all day.

1st Corps.

The 1st Corps advanced this morning from BOURG supported by the Cavalry Division on its right; the 2nd Brigade of the 1st Division was attacked near CERNY, but drove off the enemy and captured twelve guns; several hundred prisoners were also taken.

During the day both 1st and 2nd Divisions successfully drove off the hostile counter attacks and in the afternoon the 2nd Division was holding the plateau South of OSTEL supported by the 4th Cavalry Brigade on its left and the 2nd Cavalry Brigade on its right.

5th French Army On the right of the 1st Corps the 18th French Corps was heavily attacked at CRAONNELLE and has been ordered to maintain itself in its present position.

On the right of the 18th Corps the group of Reserve Divisions is at BERRY AU BAC, and with the 3rd Corps on its right holds the line of the canal through LOIVRE to LA NEUVILLETTE near REIMS. The 1st Corps occupies REIMS. The 10th Corps is on its right.

At 4.30 p.m. the French 5th Army (less the 18th Corps) were ordered to take the offensive along the whole front.

2. The Army will operate tomorrow according to instructions issued personally by the Commander-in-Chief to General Officers Commanding Corps and Cavalry Divisions.

3.

2nd sheet.

3. Supply railheads for the 15th September will be:-

1st Cavalry Division	FERE EN TARDENOIS
1st Corps	do.
G.H.Q.	do.
R.F.C.	do.
L. of C. Units.	do.
General Gough's Command	OULCHY-BRENY
2nd Corps	do.
3rd Corps	NEUILLY ST FRONT

Ammunition Parks will continue to replenish at NOGENT L'ARTAUD.

4. Reports to FERE EN TARDENOIS.

(sd.) Henry Wilson.
Lieutenant-General,
Chief of the General Staff.

Issued at

"A" Form.
MESSAGES AND SIGNALS.
Army Form C. 2121

Prefix	Code	m.	Words	Charge	This message is on a/c of:	Recd. at ____ m.
Office Origin and Service Instructions.			Sent			Date
			At ____ m.		Service.	From
			To			By
			By		(Signature of "Franking Officer.")	

TO {
4th Hussars   3rd Bde RHA   A Echelon
5th Lancers   Amm Col.   B "
16th "   2nd Cav Fd Amb.   19th Hussars

Sender's Number	Day of Month	In reply to Number	
BM 2	Sixteenth		AAA

Reference attached operation order :- ① The units of the 3rd Cav Bde will march independently to occupy the same positions as they were in yesterday by 7am ② The O.C. 4th Hussars will relieve his Squadron at CHAUSSEE by another Squadron. ③ The 2nd Cav Field Ambulance will remain at BRAYNE, keeping a Light Ambulance ready to join the Brigade should it advance. ④ The Amm. Col. and A and B Echelon 1st line Transport will remain at LIME ⑤ The machine gun detachment 19th Hussars will accompany the 16th Lancers. The remaining details 19th Hussars will remain at LIME.

From 3rd Cav Bde
Place LIME
Time 1 am

The above may be forwarded as now corrected.   (Z)   K J Brearley M of Bde
                                         Censor.   Signature of Addressor or person authorised to telegraph in his name.

Wt. W1154/2240. 7/11. 7,500,000. Sch. 4a. "A" Form. Army Form C. 2121.

MESSAGES AND SIGNALS.

TO 2^d Cav Div.

Sender's Number.	Day of Month	In reply to Number	
G.	Fifteenth.		AAA

Operation Order No. 25. 1. On the right of the British Army the French have made progress AAA The eighteenth Corps has occupied CRAONNE and the high ground on the left and is in touch with the right of our First Corps AAA On the left the French have reached the general line SOISSONS - NOYON and are making progress on their left AAA Our Army has successfully maintained its position and has repulsed numerous counter attacks inflicting severe loss on the enemy AAA The Sixth Division has to-day reached ROCOURT and is marching early to-morrow morning to join Third Corps AAA

2. The Army will assume a general offensive at the first opportunity AAA

3. The Second Corps will entrench strongly the line now held by it with the intention of assuming the offensive at the first opportunity

Wt. W1154/2240. 7/11. 7,500,000. Sch. 4a.	"A" Form.	Army Form C. 2121.
MESSAGES AND SIGNALS.		No. of Message_____

Prefix_____Code_____m.	Words	Charge	This message is on a/c of:	Recd. at_____m.
Office of Origin and Service Instructions.	Sent		_____Service.	Date_____
	At_____m.			From_____
	To_____			
	By_____		(Signature of "Franking Officer.")	By_____

TO				

Sender's Number.	Day of Month	In reply to Number	A A A

in conformity with paragraph two AAA
4. Railhead for supplies OULCHY - BRENY
Rendezvous and refilling point Third Division
BRAINE at seven a.m. Rendezvous and refilling
point Fifth Division FME DE L'EPITAPHE at seven a.m.
AAA No. Three Ammunition Park is on the main
FERE EN TARDENOIS - SOISSONS road at cross road
South of Y in OUIRY - HOUSSE with sections just
North of E in LESGES and at FME DE L'EPITAPHE AAA
Railhead for ammunition FERE EN TARDENOIS AAA
5. Reports to the CHATEAU at MURET

and acknowledge

From: Second Corps
Place
Time: 10/20 p.m.

The above may be forwarded as now corrected. (Z)

Censor. Signature of Addressor or person authorised to telegraph in his name.

* This line should be erased if not required.

Gen. Gough

SECRET.

Copy No. 5

OPERATION ORDER NO. 26
by
Field-Marshal Sir John French, G.C.B., etc.,
Commander-in-Chief, British Forces in the Field.

General Head Quarters,
15th September 1914.

1. On the right of the British Army the French have made some progress.
   The 18th Corps has occupied CRAONNE and the high ground on the left and is in touch with the right of our 1st Corps.
   On the left the French have reached the general line SOISSONS - NOYON and are making progress on their left.
   Our Army has successfully maintained its position and has repulsed numerous counter attacks inflicting severe loss on the enemy.
   The 6th Division has today reached ROCOURT and is marching early tomorrow morning to join 3rd Corps.

2. The Commander-in-Chief wishes the line now held by the Army to be strongly entrenched and it is his intention to assume a general offensive at the first opportunity.

3. Supply Railheads for the 16th September will be:-

1st Cavalry Division	FERE EN TARDENOIS
1st Corps	do.
G.H.Q.	do.
R.F.C.	do.
L. of C. Units	do.
General Gough's Command	OULCHY-BRENY
2nd Corps	do.
3rd Corps	NEUILLY ST FRONT.
Ammunition Railhead	FERE EN TARDENOIS Rly. Stn.

4. Reports to FERE EN TARDENOIS.

(Sd.) A.J.MURRAY,
Lieutenant-General,
Chief of the General Staff.

Issued at 8.30 p.m.

GENERAL HEADQUARTERS
15 SEP. 1914
O.B./B 619

3rd Cav. Bde

CONFIDENTIAL.

Copy. G.H.Q.,
19-9-14.

Dear Gough,

I have heard officially and privately from War Office that an agitation is starting in the country over the meagre lists of N.C.Os. and men killed wounded and missing.

The War Office realises the difficulties but the public do not and there is a fear that unless we can soon get more or less up to date with casualties it may effect recruiting.

Will you tell your staff to do everything possible to get units to send in such returns and rolls as they are able to make out to D.A.G., 3rd Echelon, NANTES, where they will be checked and put right as far as information allows

An effort must be made by units to get something done in this direction.

The French too are calling out about casualties to interpreters, these should come with the daily casualty telegram here (G.H.Q.).

An officer reported killed, Lt.R.T.Moore, 12th Lancers, has been found to be alive by War Office.

Yours sincerely,
(Sd) C.F.Macready.

(Adjutant General, Expeditionary Force, G.H.Q.)

Operation Orders by No. 12.
Brig-General J. Vaughan, D.S.O, Comdg 3rd Cav. Bgde.

1. The situation remains unchanged. The 2nd Cav. Divn fills the gap between the 3rd and 5th Divisions having outpost squadrons (1) blocking the CHASSEMY — CONDÉ road (2) holding the Bridge over the River VESLE, 1 mile south of CONDÉ.

2. The task of the 3rd Cav. Bgde is to find the Squadrons on the CHASSEMY — CONDÉ road with the remainder of the Regiment and a Battery in support of the 2 outpost squadrons.

3. The O.C. 4th Hussars will detail one Squadron to relieve the outpost squadron of the 5th Lancers at 6.30 a.m. and at the same hour to be in support with the remainder of his regiment. The Machine Gun detachment will accompany the outpost squadron.

"D" Battery R.H.A. will be in the position occupied by "E" Battery today by 6.30 a.m. The whole to be under the command of Major Howell 4th Hussars.

4. Remainder of the Brigade will remain in their billets ready to saddle up at a moment's notice.

5. Reports to the Chateau at LIMÉ.

LIME
17-9-14.
Issued at
6.45 pm

B H Kearsley Major.
Brigade Major.

Copy No.1

OPERATION ORDERS No.2
by
Brigadier General H.Gough,C.B.,
Commanding 2nd Cavalry Division,
BRAINE,
17th September 1914.

1. The general situation and the role of the Division remain the same as yesterday.

2. The G.O.C., 3rd Cavalry Brigade will detail 1 regiment and 1 battery to relieve those detailed by the 5th Brigade today, the relief to take place at 7 a.m. tomorrow.

3. The squadron on outpost duty will be relieved during tomorrow under brigade arrangements.

4. The remainder of the Division will stay in their present billets ready to turn out at short notice.

5. Supply rail-head - OULCHY-BRENY.
Ammunition rail-head - FERE-EN-TARDENOIS, Railway Stn.

6. Divisional Headquarters moved to BRAINE this afternoon, No.24 in the big square in the middle of the town.

W.H.GREENLY, Lieut-Colonel,
C.S.O., 2nd Cavalry Division.

By Orderly.
6-45 p.m.

O.C. 4th Hussars.   16th Lancers.
   5th Lancers   D Battn R.H.A
   A & B Echelons   2nd Cav. Fd Ambulance

B.M. 59.
   LIME. 22/9/14

Unless further orders are
received units will remain in
their present billets tomorrow

R H Keanley
   Major
   Bde. Major 3rd Cav. Bde

Issued at 7pm

4th Hussars.   2nd Cav: F.d Amb:
5th Lancers.   'A' Echelon }
16th Lancers   'B'   "   } 1st L. Transpat.
'D' B.y RHA.

B.M. 33.   Sept. 18th

The general situation today remains
unchanged.
   The army will maintain its position
tomorrow pending the resumption of a
general offensive.
   The 2nd Cav Div.n will form part of a
General Reserve under the C in C and
will remain for the present as at present
located.
   The outpost squadron will return to
billets as soon as relieved by Infantry.
   No operation orders will be issued
tonight.

                              R. H. Kearsley Maj
                                    Bde Maj
LINE.   3rd Cav B.de
10.20 pm.

Prefix	Code	m.	Words	Charge	This message is on a/c of:	Recd, at	m.
Office of Origin and Service Instructions.			Sent			Date	
			At	m.	Service.	From	
			To				
			By		(Signature of "Franking Officer.")	By	

TO: 4th Hussars, 5th Lancers, 16th Lancers, "D" By RHA, 2nd Cav Fd Amb, A & B Echelons

Sender's Number	Day of Month	In reply to Number	AAA
AM 38	Nineteenth		

Unless further orders are received the 3rd Cav: Bde will remain in its Billets tomorrow AAA.

The Revd GUINESS will hold divine Services at the following times and places.

4th Hussars - BRAINE under arrangements to be made with the O.C. 4th Hussars.

16th Lancers) Cross Roads LIME at 11 am.
D" RHA.)

5th Lancers QUINCEY at 11.45 am.

O.C. Units will please make the necessary arrangements.

From: 3rd Cav Bde
Place: LIME
Time: 6.45 pm

The above may be forwarded as now corrected. (Z) R J Kearsley Major BM.

Censor. Signature of Addressor or person authorised to telegraph in his name.
* This line should be erased if not required.

3rd Brig.   5th Brig.
OC R.H.A.   OC 4th Fd Troop

W-G. 12 Sept. 19.
 Following from G.H.Q. begins
"O.A.48 Situation today unchanged
AAA 6th Div. H.Q. are at BAZOCHES
AAA Operation orders will not be
issued unless change necessitates
ends"

                              2nd Cav. Divn
                              D H Greenly
BRAINE   C.S.O.
9.10 p.m

                                   10.10 P.m

3rd Cavalry Brigade

W.G.10.Sept.22.

    No operation orders will be issued tonight unless situation changes.

BRAINE.   Lieut-Colonel,
9 p.m.   C.S.O., 2nd Cavalry Division.

LETTER FOUND ON GERMAN OFFICER OF VII. RESERVE CORPS.

CERNY, S. OF LAON,
17-9-14.

My dear parents,

x   x   x   x

Our Corps has the task of holding the heights south of Cerny in all circumstances till the XV. Corps on our left flank can grip the enemy's flank. On our right are other corps. We are fighting with the English Guards, Highlanders, and Zouaves. The losses on both sides have been enormous. For the most part this is due to the too brilliant French artillery. The English are marvellously trained in making use of the ground. One never sees them and one is constantly under fire. The French airmen perform wonderful feats. We cannot get rid of them. As soon as an airman has flown over us, 10 minutes later we get their shrapnel fire in our position. We have little artillery in our corps; without it we cannot get forward.

Three days ago our division took possession of these heights, dug itself in, etc. Two days ago, early in the morning, we were attacked by immensely superior English forces (1 brigade and 2 battalions) and were turned out of our positions; the fellows took 5 guns from us. It was a tremendous hand to hand fight. How I escaped myself I am not clear. I then had to bring up supports on foot (my horse was wounded and the others were too far in rear). Then came up the Guard Jager Battalion (a), 4th Jager (b), 65th Regt. (c), Reserve Regt. 13 (d), Landwehr Regt. 13 (e) and 16 (e), and with help of the artillery drove back the fellows out of the position again.

Our machine guns did excellent work. The English fell in heaps.

In our battalion 3 Iron Crosses have been given, one to the C.O., one to the Captain, one to the Surgeon. Let us hope that we shall be the lucky ones next time: . . . . . During the first 2 days of the battle I had only one piece of bread, and no water, spent the night in the rain without my greatcoat. The rest of my kit was on the horses which have been left miles behind with the baggage (which cannot come up into the battle) because as soon as you put your nose out from behind cover the bullets whistle. The war is terrible. We are all hoping that the decisive battle will end the war, as our troops have already got round Paris.

If we first beat the English, the French resistance will soon be broken, Russia will be very quickly dealt with; of this there is no doubt. We received splendid help from the Austrian heavy artillery at Maubeuge. They bombarded Fort Cerfontaine in such a way that there was not 10 metres of parapet which did not show enormous craters made by shells. The armoured turrets were found upside down.

Yesterday evening about 6 p.m., in the valley in which our reserves stood, there was such a terrible cannonade that we saw nothing of the sky but a cloud of smoke.

We had few casualties.

(Remainder of letter is of no interest).

Headquarters

...3rd Cavalry Brigade....

General situation unchanged.   No operation orders will be issued tonight.

                                                 W.H. GREENLY.   LIEUT:COLONEL.
23/9/14.   G.S.O.   2nd CAVALRY DIVISION.

COPY.

2nd Cavalry Division.

O(A)156, 24 Sept.14.
Operation Orders will not be issued unless change necessitates.

G.H.Q.
8 p.m.

"A" Form.
MESSAGES AND SIGNALS.
Army Form C. 2121

This message is on a/c of:
For information

TO: 2nd Cav Div

Sender's Number: OA/161
Day of Month: 25/9/14
AAA

Turning movement of French left appears to be progressing favourably aaa The commander-in-chief anticipates a possibility of the enemy thinking the allies have unduly extended their front making a final effort to break through by an attack on some central part of the line aaa This is only a possibility but in view of it army corps commanders should be doubly careful for the next 48 hours aaa

From: A. G. Murray C.O.S
Place: GHQ
Time:

(Z) *[signature]*

3rd Cavalry Brigade.
Wanting to Complete – Sept 29th 1914.

	Personnel		Horses				
	Officers	O. Ranks	Charged	Riding	Draught	Pack	TOTAL
Bde H.Q.	—	8°	6	2	—	—	8
3rd Signal Tp.	—	5 (sig⁷)	—	5	—	—	5
4th Hussars	—	149	—	153	—	5	158
5th Lancers	6	115	—	154	8	4	166
16th Lancers	1	✳	—	12	—	1	13
D: Battery R.H.A.	—	1	—	1	—	—	1

✳ Supernumerary. 21.
◯ Includes 9 servants, which will be found from surplus 16th Lancers.

R.W.Cavalry Maj
9th

3rd Brigade

W.G.48. Sept.29.

1. The division will move tomorrow to a new billeting area in rear of the **left** flank of the army, as below:-

Divl.H.Q.   HARTENNES.

Divl.Troops.
    Ammunition Column.   PARCY-TIGNY.
    B.Echelon,Cav.Fd.Ambs.   HARTENNES.
    4th Field Troop R.E.   TAUX,1 mile N.of HARTENNES.

3rd Brigade.   AMBRIEF-CHACRISE - NAMPTEUIL -
                                                    VIOLAINE - MAAST-et-VIOLAINE.

5th Brigade.   ARCY-Ste-RESTITUE - LES CROUTTES
                                                    - DROIZY - LAUNOY - COURDOUX.

2. The 5th Brigade will march so as to be W. of the road AMBRIEF - CHACRISE - MAAST et VIOLAINE by 10 a.m.

3. Divisional Troops.
The 4th Field Troop R.E. and B Echelon of 5th Cav.Field Ambulance will march under orders to be issued by G.O.C. 5th Cav.Bde.
The Ammunition Column and B Echelon of 2nd Cav.Field Ambulance will march via 'S' of CERSEUIL,'S' of CUIRY HOUSSE and 'D' of DROIZY leaving the starting point, cross roads $\frac{1}{4}$ mile N.W. of CERSEUIL, at 9 a.m. and being clear of the CHACRISE - MAAST et VIOLAINE road by 10-15 a.m.

4. Divisional H.Q. will be at BRAINE up to 10 a.m. after which hour all messages to HARTENNES.

BRAINE.
  6-15 p.m.

2nd Cavalry Division
W.H.GREENLY,Lieut-Colonel,
C.S.O.

TO		3/ Cavalry Brigade			
Sender's Number	Day of Month		In reply to Number		
G.E. 45.	30. 9. 14.			AAA	

The under-mentioned officers and N.C.Os have been awarded the French honours, as stated below, for valuable services in the field.

Croix d'Officier

    Major J.D. Jardine, 5th Lancers
    Lieut. Col. T. Bridges, D.S.O. 4th Hussars

Croix de Chevalier

    Captain A. Neave, 16th Lancers
    Captain R.H. Sanderson R.H.A
    Captain J.K. Gatacre, I.A. att. 4th Hrs

From / Place / Time: Points 30/9/14

"A" Form.   Army Form C. 2121.
MESSAGES AND SIGNALS.

(Continued)

Medailles Militaires

N° 4441 Sergt. F. Scotcher, 4th Hussars

" 1041 Corporal W. Roberts, 5th Lancers

" 302 Sergt. E. Lawrence, 16th Lancers

" 6001 R.S.M. R.Y.K. Walker, R.H.A.

" 6632 Sergt. A. Castle, R.H.A.

To be communicated to all concerned

2/ Cav. Div.

"A" Form.			Army Form C. 2121.

MESSAGES AND SIGNALS.

TO: 3/ Cavalry Brigade

Sender's Number: G.E. 48 Day of Month: 30.9.14   AAA

Following wire received from Mil. Sec. G.H.Q

"Forward names of all officers N.C.O.s and men under your Command who are recommended for "mention in notice" despatches"

Reference above of "Subalterns" please N.C.O.s forward names and men

2/ Cav. Division

Staff Capt. Major

3rd Bde.
5th Bde.
4th Fd. Troop R E
a. D. n. S.
Amm. Col.

W.G. 50 Sept. 30

Situation unchanged: no operation orders will be issued tonight.

2nd Cav. Div.
W H Greenly, Lt Col
C. S. O.

Hartennes
6.20 pm.

Could you ask Capt Scarlett to be at ECUIRY, H.Q. 3rd Army, at 8.30 am. tomorrow to meet Gen. Gough, mounted with horse holder. WHG.

www.ingramcontent.com/pod-product-compliance
Lightning Source LLC
Chambersburg PA
CBHW080854230426
43662CB00013B/2104